THE TEMPLAR [illegible]
IN THE AGE OF AQUARIUS

THE TEMPLAR TRADITION
IN THE AGE OF AQUARIUS

GAETAN DELAFORGE

THRESHOLD BOOKS

ISBN 0-939660-17-2

LIBRARY OF CONGRESS CATALOG NUMBER: 86-051105

Illustrations courtesy of the Bibliothèque Publique Universitaire of Geneva and the Metropolitan Museum of Art, Cloisters Collection.

THRESHOLD BOOKS, RD 3, BOX 1350, PUTNEY, VERMONT 05346

CONTENTS

THE ESOTERIC TRADITION AND THE TEMPLE

THE TEMPLE IN THE AQUARIAN AGE

FOREWORD

THERE CAN BE few among us who, at some time in their life, have not gazed up at a night sky heavy with stars and asked themselves the age-old question—"Why?"

The need to give meaning to existence is not, as some earthly philosophers insist, simply the biochemical reflex action of a brain that has evolved through its ability to analyse and assign a value to the patterns of light and shade falling on the retina. It stems from some memory buried deep within us. A belief that once, in a former state of grace, we *knew* the answers; were fully aware of our role in the scheme of things and the relationship between the physical world and the spiritual realms beyond.

Sadly, many of those who turn their eyes to the heavens let the moment pass. They turn their attention back to everyday matters and become totally enmeshed in external reality. For others, that sense of wonderment is a moment of awakening, the beginning of a long journey in search of The Truth, The Light and The Way; the Shining Path that leads us upwards, back to our true beginnings in the heart of all Creation.

The road may be hard and the journey long but in order to move forward, we have to embrace two fundamental ideas: first, that each human being is endowed with a spark of the Celestial spirit, a fragment of the Godhead—what, in my own book *Mission,* I chose to call The Presence— and second, that things are not as they seem. We do indeed see "as through a glass, darkly". We must open our minds to the possibility of alternate realities, to dimensions and realms of existence beyond those defined by the laws of physics and we must reflect upon the proposition that the external world in which we are enmeshed is not the "real" world but *Maya*—illusion.

This does not mean we must abandon all worldly pursuits and pleasures. On the contrary. We must be positively engaged. But we must seek, as the Sufis urge, "to be in the world but not of it." The insights and knowledge we gain in our faltering steps along The Way must be fed back into our everyday lives in order to help bring the forces that permeate the world into balance. We do not have to carry banners or preach on street corners. By living a sane, solid existence, with a firm grasp of the eternal values, we can radiate positive energies that will work upon those around us and, by example, encourage them to reassess their own lives and beliefs—or lack of them.

That's all very well, you may say but, before we begin this search, does this "Truth" with a capital "T" exist? The answer is "Yes, it most emphatically does" but it cannot be learned from books—not even this one. The moment of illumination, by its very nature, is beyond words. These things can only be learned by direct experience. Even the most brillliantly written book dealing with the subject of awareness and spiritual development is but a pale reflection of the real thing. It bears the same relationship to the rapturous Union with the Ultimate Principle as a signpost bearing the legend "Grand Canyon" has with the majestic panorama which awaits the traveller at the end of the road.

But without the signpost, most of us would never find the way—or even be aware that there was a road which led somewhere. Hence the books, such as the one you now hold in your hands. Words are often used to beguile, to confound and mislead. We must always be wary of them. But it is also true that the right words can help us make the "connection." We don't even need to fully understand what they mean. If we are ready, the power comes through the page and triggers a response deep within us. Our slumbering soul awakens as The Light pours in. We see with a sudden, blinding clarity; we know with absolute certainty that we have stumbled across The Truth. And with that discovery comes the realisation that it is something we have always carried within us but which, for so long, has lain buried and forgotten.

For some of you, it may happen as a result of reading this book. Gaetan, I know, has written it because he was "directed" to do so. There are many paths but only One Way, and the Knights Templar are widely believed to be the guardians of the True Knowledge. Many people question the real motives of "hidden orders" but, as I have briefly outlined and Gaetan himself explains, certain information can only be revealed by direct experience. The Knights Templar believe that only those who are judged to be ready should be given the keys which will enable them to open their minds and receive the secret teachings which they have guarded down the centuries.

Gaetan Delaforge contacted me after reading *"Mission"*—a book which I also believed I had been directed to write. It became clear in the course of our several conversations that much of the material I had placed before the reader within a work of fiction was part of the body of knowledge guarded by the Knights Templar and other related spiritual traditions. Since most of what I had written had its genesis in an out-of-body experience my meetings with him confirmed my belief that this knowledge does indeed exist outside ourselves. All we have to do is tune in on the right wavelength.

Gaetan Delaforge is not the author's real name but I can assure the reader he is a very real person in every sense. His experiences along The Way which led to the writing of this book seem to be even more extraordinary and more persistent than my own, but he has, nevertheless, managed to maintain a healthy balance between this world and those beyond, and he also possesses a disarming sense of humour—something we all need when trying to come to grips with the Inner Mysteries. Holding a senior position in an international organization he was obliged to adopt a pseudonym. This is more a reflection on the nature of international organizations than on the man himself.

I commend his work to you. Read it as all books of this nature should be read, not with your eyes, but with your soul.

Patrick Tilley
North Wales/September 1986

INTRODUCTION

THIS BOOK is not a historical work and is hardly likely to appeal to those whose interest is purely intellectual. It is in fact addressed to a very particular type of individual who somewhere inside him or herself already "knows" what this book is all about.

Its purpose is to stimulate the reader for whom it is destined to join others in carrying out the time-honoured task of the Temple that lies ever latent in the heart of man, spurring him on to undertake the quest for the eternal Grail. The task of the Temple will always be the same—to work unceasingly for Man with a capital M and for a world in which Man will be able to fulfill his highest aspirations: spiritual, moral, mental and creative.

Since time immemorial the Temple has worked under various names for these goals. It has been particularly active in the dark periods of history, when it has been a source of light in ways adapted to the time, spurring humanity upwards from the darkness of ignorance, egoism, and brutality to the nobler regions of the spirit.

The best known but least understood manifestation of the Temple was that which burst upon the medieval world through the activities of the Order of the Knights Templar during the period 1118 to 1314. This order of chivalry, which swept like a comet through nearly 200 years of Christendom, was to meet its demise in calumny, torture, and martyrdom, orchestrated by that cunning and greedy ruler, King Philip the Fair of France, who in one master stroke seized the wealth of the Templars and smashed their influence. If Philip was the unconscious instrument of the powers of darkness in the eternal battle with the forces of light, he acted too late, because by then the ideals of the Templars had left their imprint not only on European life and thought, but on the spirit of men for all time.

It is not the aim of this short work to vindicate the Templars or to prove that the allegations made against them were false. This has been done by qualified historians, and interested readers will find a number of references to this aspect in the bibliography. Rather than joining in this old debate, the writer wishes to address the modern seeker of the Grail: the defender of the eternal Temple, the man or woman whose head is lifted towards the heavens in aspiration, whose feet are firmly placed on the ground, and whose heart, in the center, links head to feet and drives its possessor onwards to sacrifice his cross of illusion for the reality of spiritual illumination.

The writer is certain that this book will fall into the hands of those for whom it is intended because the Temple has always found its own. At important moments in the history of our planet, a small number of men and women have always felt the call, not only in their heads but in their hearts. Such people have relegated other preoccupations to their proper place and carried out what the Temple demanded of them—service to humanity, preparing the way so that one day "Man" with a capital M can finally manifest.

The author apologizes in advance for what might seem to be a rather concise treatment of many important subjects in the chapters which follow. If only a few readers manage to ignore imperfections in the text and respond with their hearts to what the author has tried to transmit—the call of the eternal Temple—he will have done his job.

G.D.
1985.

This book is dedicated to my mentor and friend K., without whose inspiration it would not have been written, and to all those who past, present and future strive that one day that Being called Man with a capital "M" can be realized on this planet.

THE TEMPLE AND SOME OF ITS EARLY MANIFESTATIONS

Melchisedek, from a stone sculpture at Chartres Cathedral.

CHAPTER I

THE TEMPLE, THE ORDER OF MELCHISEDEK AND THE ESSENES

The Meaning of the Temple

THE KNOWLEDGE about man's origins and the reason for his existence in the Cosmos, of which generations of initiates have been the guardians, has always remained the same in essence, though the language, the symbols and the institutions used to express this knowledge are changed or adapted to conform to the experience and needs of the civilization of the time. For example, the Judeo-Christian vision of the beginnings of life and its future on this planet and beyond is but one version of the story of man and the universe. Each civilization has had its version, each valid for the time and the people for whom it was intended. Each of these versions or traditions has had its esoteric or secret aspects. What is extraordinary, however, is that there are more similarities than differences in the methods used by these secret traditions to change the consciousness of their respective practitioners.

The word "esoteric" means hidden spiritual or philosophical teachings intended only for the initiated. The terms "Spiritual Tradition," "Primordial Tradition," "Esoteric Tradition" or simply "The Tradition" refer to that collection of esoteric knowledge, teachings or realizations which cannot be, or have not been, communicated in written form. Down the ages such knowledge has been transmitted orally or through methods known only to initiates, methods which provoke an inner realization rather than an intellectual comprehension within the seeker.

According to esoteric tradition, life manifested as the being we know as *homo sapiens* did not originate on this planet, but was implanted here by more advanced spiritual beings who came from elsewhere. Knowledge of man's true origins and the blueprint for his evolutionary destiny was periodically transmitted by these beings to humans who were sufficiently evolved to receive this knowledge. The latter, generally known in the tradition as "initiates," have kept the knowledge intact by passing it on to worthy successors.

Man has always believed that there should be a special place dedicated to the reception of higher knowledge, and all great spiritual traditions have encouraged respect and veneration for the place or building where contact with a higher level of consciousness, the source of transcendental knowledge, —divinity, the gods, God or the ultimate creator—was sought. The Latin word *templum* from which the word temple derives, signifies a holy enclosure or building screened from the eyes of the profane. In later times it came to mean a shrine where people worshipped, whatever the denomination; it was also used in fraternal orders like the Freemasons to designate a place in their lodges where their ceremonies took place. Esoterically the temple symbolizes the receptacle in which divine revelation is received. It is also a material representation of the human heart, which is the true temple. According to the Tradition, the physical temple is only necessary because at the present stage of evolution, the majority of mankind cannot contact higher levels of consciousness without external aids. This is gradually changing now that we have entered the Age of Aquarius.

One of the elements of knowledge handed down over the ages was how to build temples. These places, destined for contact with higher intelligences, angels, gods, or simply the divine, were not built just anywhere. It is now known that they were quite often erected where the location favoured a junction between cosmic and telluric currents.

Sometimes nearness to a depression with underground

water, or to a hill with a particular shape was considered desirable. The Templars learned in the Middle East about the science of energies for building and used it to revolutionize the art of cathedral construction in Europe. The Roman Catholic church apparently retained knowledge of the art, and used it in building churches up to the Reformation. The purpose of all these techniques was to ensure that something happened during ceremonies—that some kind of transmission of spiritual knowledge or realization took place for the benefit of those present.

Esoteric tradition has used the word 'temple' in a wide sense. The Tradition itself as a repository of primordial wisdom has been called the Temple. It is from this point of view that any spiritual movement which in its deeper teachings respects the purity of the primordial wisdom handed down by initiates, can be considered to be a manifestation of the true and eternal Temple.

The Order Of Melchisedek

One documented account of an early example of the transmission of spiritual knowledge is the Bible's reference to the meeting between the patriarch Abraham and the mysterious Melchisedek.

The name Melchisedek is derived from the Hebrew Melki Tzaddiq, King or Ruler of Righteousness. Very little is known about this legendary personage. Reference is made to him in the Bible as follows:

And Melchisedek King of Salem brought forth bread and wine; and he was the priest of the most high God.

And he blessed him, and said, Blessed be Abram of the most high God possessor of heaven and earth.

And blessed be the most high God, which hath delivered thine enemies into thy hand. And he gave him tithes of all.

(Genesis 14, 18-20)

The Lord hath sworn, and will not repent, Thou art a priest for ever after the order of Melchisedek.

(Psalms 110, 4)

For this Melchisedek, King of Salem, priest of the most high God, who met Abraham returning from the slaughter of the kings, and blessed him;

To whom also Abraham gave a tenth part of all; first being by interpretation King of righteousness, and after that also King of Salem, which is, King of peace;

Without father, without mother, without descent, having neither beginning of days, nor end of life; but made like unto the son of God; abideth a priest continually.

Now consider how great this man was, unto whom even the patriarch Abraham gave the tenth of the spoils.

And it is yet far more evident; for that after the similitude of Melchisedek there ariseth another priest,

Who is made, not after the law of a carnal commandment, but after the power of an endless life.

For those priests were made without an oath, but this with an oath by him that said unto him, The Lord sware and will not repent, Thou art a priest for ever after the order of Melchisedek .

(Hebrews 7, 1-21).

Templar teachings shed light on the meaning of some of these citations. For example, according to the biblical narrative, Melchisedek was born without father or mother. To the Templars this means that Melchisedek was not born on this planet, but was an advanced spiritual being who came from elsewhere. The Bible states that Melchisedek gave Abraham bread and wine after the latter had conquered the Kings of Edom. In Templar tradition this relates to a symbolic act of the highest importance.

The giving of bread and wine to Abraham is just another way of saying that because Abraham had conquered the warring elements in himself, he had reached the stage where he was ready to take another step on the ladder of evolution. By direct transmission of some kind, Melchisedek initiated

Abraham into a new level of consciousness and awareness.

One of the tasks assigned to the original Templars was to encourage the unification of Islam and Christianity. Such a realization would in a way be a return to the original source of revelation which gave birth to these two great religions. Melchisedek transmitted the essence of the Tradition to Abraham, who in turn passed it on to his sons, Isaac and Ishmael.

From age to age this deposit of spiritual knowledge has come down to us in two streams, one through Israel (Moses), and the other through the African and Arabian initiates (Jethro). The two strands were brought together for the first time by Moses after he was initiated in the Egyptian mysteries.

The Essenes, with their Egyptian links, collaborated with John the Baptist to prepare the coming of the Christ, bringing together the two currents once again. After the Christ the two branches resumed their parallel routes, one of which produced Mohammed, another great manifestation of the divine spirit.

To the Templars, therefore, Melchisedek is one of the key symbols of the Order of the Temple. He is a father figure in the same way that Hiram Abiff is the father figure in the tradition of Freemasonry. At Chartres, one of the great French cathedrals, whose construction was sponsored by the Templars, an impressive stone carving and a beautiful stained glass window pay homage to Melchisedek, father of the eternal priesthood.

According to Templar tradition, Melchisedek was neither born in the normal sense " . . . having neither beginning of days, nor end of life; . . ." nor did he die. This great manifestation of the divine did not need to die. His mission was not the same as that of the other archetype—the Christ. Melchisedek symbolized the eternal spirit of the Father aspect of the Godhead, while the Christ symbolized the principle of the Son. As the archetype of the Son, the Christ had to incarnate and conquer death to prove to a sceptical humanity that life was indeed eternal.

Two symbols have been associated with Melchisedek—wheat and the beehive. Wheat symbolizes nourishment, spiritual and physical. The beehive is a symbol of unity, where many parts work for the good of the whole. The six-sided cell of the honey bee is also representative of the six-rayed star—the star of David—which also symbolizes esoterically the perfect union of the lower and higher aspects of man, the conjunction of two triangles.

Melchisedek, founder of the priesthood for the Western Tradition, was described in the biblical texts quoted earlier as King of Salem. The name Salem is apparently derived from the Hebrew word Shalom, meaning peace. Later on in Chapter III on the Cosmic Christ, an attempt is made to clarify why opposition is inevitable and in some way necessary at the present level of evolution of our planet. It is therefore interesting to observe that in the city of Jerusalem there is perpetual confrontation between the two branches of Abraham's descendants—that of Sarah, which was to produce the Christ, and that of Hagar, from whom descended Mohammed, the founder of Islam.

It should be clear from what is said above that the Order of Melchisedek does not exist on a material level. Any person who has reached the level of spiritual advancement where he can make conscious contact with the roots of our spiritual tradition is *de facto* a member of the Order of Melchisedek. Any priest who by his spiritual capacity is able to function as a channel for the spiritual energies of the Christ, is a priest after the Order of Melchisedek.

Another outstanding example of spiritual transmission in biblical history was the giving of bread and wine by the Christ to his disciples at the Last Supper. The historic words of the Christ in St. Luke 22, 19: "And he took bread, and gave thanks, and gave unto them, saying 'This is my body which is given for you; this do in remembrance of me,'" meant that the disciples were instructed to perpetuate this act in the future. Ordained priests are supposed to have inherited the tradition of transmission by which they should be able to stimulate a new awareness of spiritual realities during the Eucharistic moment of the Mass when the host and the wine are consecrated. Either recipients are particularly secretive about their experiences or something has been lost, since these days one does not meet many people who say that the level of their consciousness has been raised after taking communion. Perhaps the ecclesiastic tradition has left out in its training for the ministry those techniques which Abraham and subsequent initiates may have used to ensure victory over the "Kings of Edom" within themselves before attempting to transmit divine knowledge and consciousness.

The Essenes

The Essenes were members of an esoteric order which was born and developed during the two centuries which preceded the capture of Jerusalem by Titus and the period until the destruction of the second Temple about 70 AD. The discovery of the Qumran manuscripts in 1947 brought a considerable amount of information about this ancient sect to the notice of the general public. Non-esoteric circles have begun to realize that the influence of the Essenes on early Christianity was far greater than at first imagined. Some of these manuscripts can be seen today in a museum built especially to house them in Jerusalem.

The etymology of the word Essene is disputed among experts. It is generally believed to have originally derived from a word which meant holy or saintly. There is reason to believe that the teachings and practices of the Essenes were of Egyptian origin. According to tradition, at the time of Jesus there existed three religious sects among the Jews in the Holy Land—the Pharisees, the Saducees and the Essenes. Some historians believe that Jesus was an Essene because while he denounced the errors of the two other sects, he never criticized nor even mentioned the Essenes. They further support this belief by observing that many of the precepts of the New Testament coincide with the teachings of the Essenes. The Temple tradition asserts that both Jesus and his parents were Essenes.

The Essenes were strict in the observance of their rules and lived a very pure life. They inhabited a separate community near the Dead Sea to avoid contamination and to await the coming of the "Messiah."

Their observance of the communion and the sharing of bread, which as we have seen was first attributed to Melchisedek, has made the memory of these pure men and women much venerated by the Order of the Temple, which considers the Essenes to have been the heirs and guardians of the priesthood of Melchisedek.

Worship originally revolved around the offering of blood, which traditionally was believed to be the carrier of the life force in man. When this was presented to the Divine, man considered that he was offering his most valuable gift—life itself. He hoped thereby that the object of his worship would reciprocate by permitting him to share in unity of a higher order. The substitution of bread and wine did not change this approach to worship. Bread and wine were the result of a whole series of efforts by man and Nature in the harsh and arid soil of Palestine, and were therefore considered to be the best of Nature.

Bread was vital for survival in those times. No wonder it was considered a gift worthy of the Creator. Wine was evocative not only because of its color, but it was also seen to symbolize and express the very life force of Nature. Thus when these two elements of material life were presented to Divinity, man expected that in exchange these offerings would be spiritualized, so that in consuming them he would share the nature of the Divine.

Over the centuries there have been people charged with

the progressive refinement of the material preparations for the communion rite. Whether they were consciously aware of it or not, the whole objective of the exercise was to realize Cosmic Unity. It is interesting to note that the host of the communion service is round—and the circle is the symbol of unity.

The ceremony instituted by Melchisedek represented the Old Covenant between man and the Divine, whereby bread and wine symbolized the essence of the earth. The Eucharist, which is the name given to the communion ceremony first performed by the Christ at the Passover Feast, represents the New Covenant. It is believed that in the ceremony of the Eucharist, the solar energy of the Christ force descends to act as an intermediary so that to the extent of their spiritual possibilities, worshippers will be enabled to approach closer to the Unity of all life.

The important part played by the Essenes in preserving the basic message and thoughts associated with these ideas, and in preparing the ground for the New Covenant, was recognized and commemorated by the Templars. Eclectic as they were, the Templars were certainly influenced by the Essenes in their teachings and practices. Some modern Templar orders include a rite in their ceremonies known as the Essene Rite not only because of its historic associations, but also because the important part of the ceremony is the breaking and sharing of a loaf of bread by all present. The act of men and women gathering together consciously to share one of Nature's most precious gifts in a moment of unity, is considered by Templars to be a symbolic affirmation of the very essence of the tradition of the Temple. Thus although the notion of sacrifice which characterizes the Eucharist is not present in this rite, it is a unifying ceremony which seeks to reinforce the links between man and his fellow beings and between man and the Divine.

BASIC TEACHINGS AND SYMBOLS OF THE TEMPLE

CHAPTER II
THE HOLY GRAIL

SYMBOLS ARE PART and parcel of the human psyche and are of the highest spiritual and psychological importance. They dwell in our subconscious where they serve as accumulators of psychic energies. When set in motion these can have far-reaching effects on our lives, not only in terms of how we perceive reality, but also in motivating us to various kinds of action. Symbols can be manipulated by us or by others in order to change our perception of ourselves and the world around us.

Modern psychoanalysts, such as the Swiss Carl Jung, have confirmed what was always known to initiates, that in addition to our individual symbols, there are symbols of great power which dwell in the subconscious of the race, or what Jung has christened the collective unconscious. These collective symbols, also called archetypes, act and interact with individuals, regions and nations, influencing our aspirations, feelings and culture. Some of these archetypes are extremely positive in bringing about psychological wholeness or greater spiritual awareness.

Closely linked to these collective archetypes are certain cultural phenomena known as myths. A myth can be defined as a fictitious narrative which can express certain truths, usually in dramatic form. Often the story which gave rise to a particular myth was based on certain actions which did take place, but which over time became dramatized by succeeding generations of narrators. It is as if certain archetypes became gradually superimposed on particular myths. Archetypes continually seek to express themselves through human beings, and the collective imagination willingly assists in this activity.

In certain cases there is such an interaction between the archetypal symbol and the myth that after several generations people no longer differentiate between the symbol and the myth.

The Egyptian triad of Osiris, Isis and Horus are very evocative symbols, and are used in meditation in many schools of esoteric teachings. Historians are not certain whether they actually lived, whether they were rulers who were deified after their deaths by popular imagination, or were personalities completely created by legend. Today it is not important whether they existed or not. They have become psychological realities thanks to the power of the archetypes and as such they can influence our inner world if we know how to approach them.

Anyone wishing to demonstrate for himself the validity of the above statement has only to select a set of positive symbols from any of the great spiritual traditions and meditate regularly on their meaning. He or she will be surprised at the effect these symbols will have on their inner life. The only precondition is that symbols from different traditions should not be mixed and the symbols should be given at least a month to gestate in the subconscious before results can be expected.

The Grail is one of the most important symbols in the tradition of the Order of the Temple. The story of King Arthur, his Knights of the Round Table and their search for the Holy Grail is part of the mythology of Western culture. To most Western people, the mere mention of the quest for the Holy Grail touches deep well-springs of awe and nobility in the subconscious.

Many books have been written about the Grail and a number of these are listed in the bibliography. It is not the intention here even to attempt a synthesis of literature about the Grail, but rather by evoking a number of ideas to stimulate the reader to become aware of the spiritual reality of the Grail. Reference was made above to myths and the interaction between myths and symbols. The Grail is without doubt one of the most powerful symbols which exists. From the experience of the writer, it is impossible to meditate regularly on its symbolism without feeling powerful effects on one's inner and outer life. Indeed, so powerful is this symbol that those who, like Parsifal, have the spiritual and psychic sensitivity to respond to it, can find that their lives are affected dramatically (to say the least). Individuals of this kind are indeed born Knights of the Holy Grail. Why some people should be more endowed in this respect than others is a long story. The answer to this and many other seeming enigmas will be found by the true seeker of the Grail, whether he is a born knight or merely a humble sword-bearer. The writer can guarantee that the how and the why will be revealed to the sincere seeker who undertakes the Grail quest by dedicating himself to the ideal of spiritual self-discovery and, above all, to the service of humanity.

All spiritual traditions give various versions or interpretations of the Grail story, in which the hero sets out on a quest. In some, including the Western tradition, the Grail is symbolized by a cup, while in others it is a stone or a dish. In all cases, however, the object is some kind of receptacle into which the essence of spiritual realization is placed for safekeeping and for transmission to the worthy. Some traditions claim that real physical objects are involved; others state that a material object which over centuries has been revered as the Grail eventually takes on the qualities of the symbolic Grail. Yet another view is that the Grail is a powerful archetype which exists in the fourth dimension, and which because of its importance for the evolution of humanity is particularly susceptible to solicitation from those who possess the necessary sensitivity and whose everyday lives express sacrifice for the divine ideal. According to this school of thought, in the condition just described, the archetypal Grail could ensoul an object such as a chalice or a cup, or even in certain special situations manifest itself to people in a vision. From the writer's experience, there is something in all these assertions. How much of all this is physical reality, symbolism, or something in between, the reader is invited to find out for himself. It is much more exciting and effective to find out certain things for oneself and, who knows, one might find out that reality is stranger than fiction.

Some people believe that the viewpoints mentioned above could explain some of the legends about the Grail. There is, for example, the legend of the cup which Joseph of Arimathea was said to have used to collect the blood of the Christ, and which centuries later made its way to the Cathar country in France. The story goes that at one stage it was carried to the provinces of Aragon, Huesca and Navarra in northern Spain for safe-keeping, after which it disappeared. A replica is kept today in the Cathedral of Valencia. Another version is that the Grail eventually reached England where, after a stay at Glastonbury, it also disappeared. In certain esoteric circles there have been hints that there are places on our planet where the vibratory conditions are such that the seeker may more easily contact the spiritual realities symbolized by the Grail. Nowadays the veils which have been held over certain teachings are being lifted, and with a bit of work on himself, some patience and perseverance, the seeker will undoubtedly be rewarded.

It is interesting to reflect that although Christian doctrine has taken many concepts and symbols which were pre-Christian into its fold, the Grail has never been adopted by orthodoxy. Nevertheless, the Grail, with its strong links to Celtic and even older mythology, managed somehow to exist in the background and was never condemned, even during the period when there was strong opposition to anything which was remotely pagan in origin.

The Grail as a cup or chalice is said to represent the feminine polarity of spirituality. If wine is present in it, this is taken to symbolize the presence of the male or active principle, the two polarities—masculine and feminine, positive and negative—symbolizing perfect manifestation. The feminine principle in life was not given the same consideration in Western civilization as the male principle, despite the addition of the symbol of the Virgin Mary to church doctrine. The adoption of Protestantism as a state religion in some countries diminished its importance still further. The Grail legend, symbolized as a receptive feminine archetype in the collective unconscious, has helped to preserve the feminine principle in man's consciousness, especially during the period of the Reformation which experienced the strong masculine influences of Lutheranism and Calvinism.

In recent centuries our civilization has tended to overemphasize the masculine principle, and the balancing force of the feminine is now due to manifest in order to rectify this tendency. It can safely be predicted that the Grail mystery with the feminine symbol of the cup or chalice will again take hold of the popular imagination and fulfil its primordial destiny.

In the light of what has been said in the preceding paragraphs, could one give a simple reply to the question of what the Grail really is? One answer might be that the Grail is the symbolic representation of what man will discover about himself and about the real meaning of life in his search for truth. The Grail is the essence of all that is, and is yet to be manifested. It can therefore never be fully comprehended, since life in the Cosmos will never end. At our limited level of understanding the Grail can be regarded symbolically as the perfect blueprint of what Man is intended to be at the summit of his evolution on the planet Earth.

CHAPTER III

THE COSMIC CHRIST

THE MODERN MIND, especially that of today's youth, is turned off rather than dynamized when the word Christ is mentioned. This is due, no doubt, largely to the failings of the established church, which continues to present the Christ as the meek, emasculated "do-gooder" carpenter of Nazareth, and the teachings he left behind as vague exhortations without obvious practical possibilities for changing people and their lives. Nowadays, all kinds of groups and sects claim that their techniques, if applied regularly, will bring demonstrable results. On the other hand, to most young people church services never seem to achieve anything except to induce yawns and boredom. Established religion does not give them something that can be seen to work or to bring peace and fulfillment in the here and now, whereas other approaches such as the Eastern tradition claim they can do all this and more.

The Order of the Temple, like other bearers of the Western esoteric spiritual tradition, has always taught a completely different version of what the Christ really is. The church has doubly failed in its duty because at this moment in the 1980s the current generation is better placed than at any time in our history to appreciate the esoteric presentation of that great cosmic being—the Christ. The era of space travel will help in enabling the general public to realize that the saga of life in the Cosmos could not begin and end with the speck of dust which we call Earth. Of course, our bit of cosmic dust is of vital importance to us, and as such (as we have and will continue to stress) has to be cherished and loved. On the other hand, this should not oblige us to place medieval blinders on our mental and spiritual eyes.

The purely historical version of what the Christ really was and is must strike anyone who is not literally asleep as being completely inadequate. Given the intellectual development of people in the Palestine of 2000 years ago, how could one have explained television or air travel to them? The Bible relates great spiritual truths, but it was written in the language and concepts of the time. It is up to us to re-examine its teachings within the wider understanding of the general knowledge we have today. We will find that its essential truths are still valid, but looked at from the wider factual perspective of today, its teachings convey to us realizations of vaster significance than they could to the more primitive minds of our forefathers. In the same way, future generations will have a broader conception of the Bible's basic truths than does ours.

The Bible itself clearly states that the Christ was a being whose life span was not limited to a mere thirty-three years. ". . . Lo, I am with you always, even unto the end of the world."(Matthew 28, 20). Also " . . . Before Abraham was, I am." (John 8, 58). The Bible further intimates that the Christ existed before the creation of our planet: "And now, O Father, glorify Thou me with Thine own self with the glory which I had with Thee before the world was." (John 17, 5). Again, " . . . for Thou lovedst me before the foundation of the world" (John 17, 24).

Today in the 1980s, it is time to abandon the idea of the crucified Christ which has hypnotized the minds of men for centuries. The concepts we should associate with the Christ in this modern age are resurrection, life and light—attributes he brought to this planet. At least some branches of the eastern Orthodox Church have indicated this direction by ending the Divine Liturgy on the joyful affirmation that "Christ is risen." In fact the rites of the Orthodox Church are closer to the source, being happy events and not the sad and sombre affairs which one finds among many denominations. In line with the approach of this book, we will limit ourselves to giving the basic teaching about the Christ as it is taught in the esoteric tradition. We will try to avoid detailed explanations, as once again our purpose is not to stimulate intellectual reflection, but rather to set off a resonance in the hearts and souls of seekers of the true Temple.

All great spiritual traditions teach that the goal of spiritual aspiration is the realization of Unity—the unity of all things and of all life throughout the entire manifested universe. The state of consciousness in which one realizes the essential unity of all things, while remaining simultaneously aware of the diversity of life, cannot be understood or demonstrated intellectually. It has to be experienced. There is enough documentary evidence available nowadays about people who have temporarily or permanently realized this state of consciousness to indicate that it is not an invention.

Many people have difficulty in accepting the assertion that the three aspects of the Godhead—the Father, the Son and the Holy Spirit—are but different manifestations of one and the same reality. If certain human beings have managed to realize their oneness with all things and with the sustainer of all life, we should not find it too difficult to conceive of the great source of life and consciousness as manifesting itself with different qualities, at different levels of energies and life impulses, which operate in ways we can identify as fatherlike, sonlike and motherlike. What is so strange about the idea of the Creator canalizing these qualities and energies through a hierarchy of beings, ranging from those whose consciousness spans a whole galaxy all the way down the scale to ordinary John Brown and Mary Smith? The Christ was and is a cosmic being of immense power through whom enormous life forces and impulses are transmitted. Each of us human beings at our microscopic level is a transmitter of cosmic forces which are being stepped down for us by beings higher up the scale.

As was mentioned in the Bible quotations above, the Christ was involved with our planet from its very creation. The Cosmic Christ is a highly evolved being who accepted the mission to guide the evolution of the Earth to the level determined by Cosmic Intelligence. The Christ is the sum total of all evolution which has taken place within our solar system. His body could be regarded as consisting of vibrations stepped down from the vast powerhouse of the Father or Universal Consciousness, so that it can be withstood and manifested by lower forms of life (including man) which draw sustenance and life from it. Periodically, whenever a new evolutionary impulse was required on the planet, the Cosmic Christ would ensoul certain individuals to various degrees. Although the influence of the Cosmic Christ can be perceived behind the great avatars of the past, the greatest influx of Light, Life and Energy of the Cosmic Christ to be injected into our planet since its creation came through the Nazarene Jesus. In order to better appreciate the mission of the Cosmic Christ, an attempt is made in the following paragraphs to summarize a number of complicated ideas.

The process of manifestation involves the creative impulse descending and expressing itself through various levels of life from the most refined to the most material, and then ascending upwards back to the source, taking with it the essence of the experiences gained. In another creative cycle it issues forth again, the process continuing eternally. Each time the creative impulse descends from Unity into manifestation it can express itself in more complicated and interesting life forms because of past experiences in earlier cycles.

Without getting involved in the deep waters of metaphysics, one could say that there is a timetable or Divine

Plan for the descent and return of the creative impulse. However, because of the existence of autonomy or free will in man, there could be a risk that without occasional adjustments, the timetable might not be completely respected. One side effect of such a cosmic accident could be the freezing of the development of a given life wave for thousands of years.

Prior to the birth of Jesus, the planet had seen the evolutionary impulse descend to its lowest ebb. According to esoteric tradition, the situation was so critical that drastic action was required. Hitherto, the Cosmic Christ had been radiating his influence in the form of light and energy to our planet without physical contact. He was now obliged to bring to earth the vast energies he represented by physical descent into material life. In order for the reader to appreciate the extent of the sacrifice involved, he should imagine what his feelings might be if he were asked to incarnate as a fly to assist the evolution of that species.

According to esoteric teachings, the descent of such a vast cosmic force could not be achieved through normal birth. A fully mature human being had to be found whose physical, emotional, mental and spiritual vehicles were sufficiently pure and strong to sustain such a force. Esoteric tradition teaches that consciousness manifests through co-ordinated forms or vehicles of varying degrees of density. In the case of a human being, the physical body is the vehicle which enables him or her to contact the world of matter, which is the densest level of manifestation on this planet. Man has other vehicles which, when developed, enable him to become aware of more subtle levels of existence.

Jesus of Nazareth and his family were members of the Essene brotherhood described in Chapter I. Jesus was trained from birth by the Essenes to carry out the mission of developing his vehicles so that they could be used to manifest the energies of the Cosmic Christ, and during his baptism by John in the river Jordan, the vehicles of Jesus were taken over by the Christ force. The being who emerged from the water became, by symbiosis, Jesus Christ—God in man—the first time this had taken place in the planet's history. The Christ knew that in order for him to carry out his mission he had to experience in his borrowed vehicles all the suffering to which human beings are subjected. If we read the New Testament's account of the Betrayal, the Crucifixion and the Resurrection from this perspective, many things will become clear.

In the garden of Gethsemane the Christ underwent the terrible ordeal of opening his vehicles to the full impact of all the evil which existed on the planet at that time. This was one of his essential tasks as a saviour of the Divine evolutionary impulse. He had to transmute the negative energies of our planet so that a balance between the forces of matter or devolution and the positive cosmic forces of the spirit or evolution could be attained. Evidently, this act of transmutation did not mean that material expression in terms of desires, motivations, et cetera, was eliminated. This was not the aim; matter was needed for the continuation of evolution on our planet. The task of the Christ was to spiritualize matter in order for it to be an instrument and servant of the spirit.

The Christ then proceeded to set the seal on the act of transformation he had performed on the emotional, mental and spiritual levels of the planet in Gethsemane. He now had to extend this process to the physical itself. He did this by giving up his life on the cross in such a way that his blood, the carrier of his cosmic energies, actually penetrated the physical earth. The fact that his side was pierced by the spear of a Roman soldier was no mere accident. No wonder legend has it that henceforth that particular spear became a spear of power. There are stories that during the Second World War, Nazi leaders tried to find this spear, which they believed to have found its way to Europe. Hitler's followers of course believed that the energy picked up by the spear could be used for their own purposes by those who knew how.

Giving up his life and blood was not enough for the Christ to accomplish the cosmic mission. After all, men before and after him had sacrificed their lives for spiritual ideals. The Christ had brought more energy to the planet than any other being before him, but for his sacrifice to be really meaningful to Man he had to suffer as a man. Thus, while suspended on the cross, he had to give up the consciousness and divine powers of a solar being and suffer as a man with all the terrible limitations which this implied. He had to endure the suffering of the crucifixion in his very flesh without the reassuring perspective of cosmic consciousness. He also had to undergo the sorrow of being pilloried in matter, helpless and cut off from his links with the Father. The anguish of this state of helplessness is recorded in the eternal words "Eli, Eli, lama sabachthani," translated as "My God, my God, why hast Thou forsaken me?" It is certain that the suffering from being cut off from his links with the heavenly world was more painful to the Christ than the physical crucifixion itself.

The way of redemption was thus established for all men, because a Cosmic and Divine Spirit had suffered as a man, and had shown through the resurrection that Man would be able to meet suffering face to face and like the Christ also conquer death. In spite of all this, the sacrifice of the Christ was still not complete. In Matthew 28, 20 the Christ declared " . . . lo, I am with you always, even unto the end of the world . . . ." The energy of the Christ is still implanted in our planet. The force and consciousness which the Christ had injected into the very particles of our Earth has now to be liberated by Man through the spiritualization of matter. Thus this cosmic energy, enriched by experience in physical manifestation, will return to its source when matter is mastered and transcended by Man through living the life taught by the Christ.

All humans beings, especially those born to respond to the call of the Temple, have a duty to participate actively in this work of redemption. Every effort by each of us to live a Christ-like life is an easing of the ties which bind this great entity to matter. Esoteric tradition does not claim that every individual unit will have to reach the level of Christ consciousness for the planet to be redeemed. What is required is a certain concentration of "redeemed consciousness" which will pull upwards those additional units which will allow themselves to be raised. This concentration can be arrived at by large numbers of people reaching a certain level or by a smaller number reaching a very high level. There is today in the 1980s a great acceleration of pollution, both of the planet and of men's minds. Unless a sufficient number of people reach the required level relatively quickly, we risk periods of great upheavals, physical, geological, social, and otherwise. In other words, the energies of the Christ must be permitted to continue their work of redemption without being unduly hindered by the abnormal density of the current material and mental environment of our planet.

The achievement of the desired level of spiritual integration and consequent redemption of the planet will lead to what the Bible describes as the Second Coming of Christ. This does not mean of course that he will return in a physical body. His Second Coming will be the coming together once again of the energies and consciousness he brought to our planet, and which are at work in all living things. This coming together will be the conscious realization of cosmic consciousness or unity by the required number of individuals.

Each of the important events which marked the life of the Christ is significant on several levels. For example, let us consider the Last Supper. The ceremony of sharing bread and wine had been practised since the times of Abraham, but since the Christ participated in the Last Supper, a new dimension was brought into the rite. Henceforth, whenever the Eucharist is performed by a priest worthy of the name, the officiant is directly linked to the cosmic force of the Christ. An automatic act of spiritual alchemy then takes place by which a certain degree of Christ force will be manifested, stimulating into activity the Christ potential present in those participating in the rite. If a Mass is performed with awareness by priests and devotees, the effect on the participants of this transmission of Christ energy can sometimes be quite powerful. Certain sensitive people have been known to be moved to the point of tears or even to faint under the impact of this cosmic force. If the Mass were performed today as originally intended, it is likely that many young people would be enabled to touch higher levels of spiritual awareness without having to resort to drugs. From this point of view, it could be said that the drug problem today is partly a reflection of the failure of traditional religion to exercise its real function of putting the faithful in touch with transcendental reality. Many who use drugs to reach "highs" or altered states of consciousness are seeking *unconsciously* to placate the nostalgia and desire of their souls for Unity with the Divine.

The ancients used the word alchemy to describe a particular system of spiritual discipline. In alchemy different constituents of the human psyche or different levels of consciousness were symbolized by certain properties such as mercury, salt, sulphur and lead. The alchemical tradition states that by manipulating the mixture of these substances in certain ways, purification will occur, permitting the realization of cosmic unity (symbolized by gold). In order for the process to work, heat has to be applied at a certain stage. To the true alchemist heat symbolizes effort, sacrifice and suffering. To raise consciousness there has to be effort and sacrifice, and when this reaches a certain level or "temperature," the gold of illumination brought about by the alchemical marriage between our lower and our spiritual selves is obtained.

The aim of this digression into alchemy is an attempt to underline the spiritual law that there can be no lasting progress without the heat of effort. Those who try to cheat this law by taking drugs frequently end up blowing a fuse, or rapidly burn up whatever spiritual capital they might have accumulated. Unless the drug taker allows time for his psychic organism to cool down and recharge itself, the desired "high" can only be recaptured by bigger and bigger doses with the risk of breakdown and death. Much pain and suffering could have been avoided by drug victims and their families if the church had been able to demonstrate to people that there are natural and more satisfying ways of fulfilling those powerful drives which push many to take drugs, ways which leave no place for the boredom, frustration and feelings of hopelessness which lead so many to search for "kicks." Thousands of adolescents could thus have been saved from psychic, moral and physical bankruptcy, and helped instead to discover fulfillment, knowledge and high adventure.

From what has been said above concerning the alchemical process, it should now be clearer why instead of banishing evil from the world during the agony of Gethsemane, the Christ limited himself to restoring the balance between the positive forces of evolution we have come to call good, and the negative, devolutionary and limitative forces of matter which we call evil. Without opposition and without struggle there is no evolution. It is certain that if the subject of suffering and the importance of effort were understood—not just intellectually, but realized and accepted—our sorrows, heartbreaks, physical pain and momentary despair would take on a new perspective, bringing something positive to our lives. Without effort and sacrifice our lives would have no meaning. Imagine for a moment that you needed only to think about anything you wanted or desired to find it there in front of you in a matter of seconds. What a bore life would be. All those who have achieved great things—artists, musicians, athletes—come to know the meaning of effort, discipline, sacrifice and suffering. It can be physical suffering for the athlete whose muscles hurt from the effort he has exerted to push himself beyond what he thought were his limits. If he aims at being a champion, his suffering can be psychological as well. He will have to undergo deprivations of all kinds, self-doubt, disappointments and setbacks, sometimes even being abandoned by those he loves because he is not always available. Like an Olympic champion, the spiritual athlete will need among other things to apply dedication, discipline, will, patience, courage, perseverance and acceptance.

There is an interesting corollary to all this. Everything we do, even the way we brush our teeth, is important spiritually. To the Cosmic Intelligence any movement is part of the process we call life. Consequently brushing one's teeth has the same importance as building a skyscraper or writing a philosophical treatise. The important thing is that the gesture of brushing or the act of building is done to the best of one's ability. There is a perfect way of performing each action in life. This perfect way exists potentially since in the divine mind the creative impulse has already conceived of how all things should be. If we do things well, we approach the archetype for that action, thus enabling that much more of the divine imprint or creative impulse to be realized, contributing thereby to the evolution of our planet and our species.

If we approached all our problems from this point of view, we would eventually end up being successful at whatever we undertook in life, whether spiritual or material. The reason for this is twofold. Firstly, doing a job well will inevitably bring rewards in the ordinary course of things. Secondly, if we act in the spirit being advocated here, the positive forces of life will be obliged to flow with us. This could not be otherwise. The life principle has but one desire, to find the best molds, channels or agents which will enable it to manifest itself.

For those who ask the question as to why the Creator

should allow evil and suffering in the world, reflection on the preceding paragraphs should help in finding some answers. At our present level of evolution, without so-called evil there would be no suffering, no need for effort, no movement, no development. We would be eternal children, happy in a kind of semi-conscious dream state. This does not mean that one should become a masochist to evolve spiritually. Some unbalanced monks seem to have believed this in medieval times and ended up as madmen for their pains. For reasons best known to the Creator, in our world effort seems to be the element which provides the motive power for growth. One might say that this is scant comfort to someone who has just lost his job, or whose spouse or only child has been killed in an accident. The answer to this is that it is we ourselves who attract suffering because some aspect of our spiritual life needs to grow. The fascinating thing about this phenomenon is that once we accept the suffering as a necessary thing, the circumstances of our lives must change. One suffers because one refuses to accept a painful situation. This suffering or resistance is the alchemical fire or heat which will burn until the life force, finding no further resistance, purifies the psyche and moves on.

There is of course another dimension to the problem which, because of its complexity, will only be touched on here. This is the law of cause and effect, which is one of the fundamental principles of esoteric teaching. According to this law, the Creator does not punish human beings for the sins they commit. An impersonal law operates in human affairs, whereby human beings are born and according to how they live their lives, lessons not learnt, or to put it differently, growth not achieved by the soul, will have to be faced as often as necessary until the message is understood and assimilated by the soul. Under this law each soul is given just the lessons it needs; no more, no less. According to this teaching, there is consequently perfect spiritual justice in the world because no one is given more suffering than he or she is due or can bear. Those who commit suicide, for example, are merely exercising their free will in turning aside from a difficult challenge, one which will have to be faced sooner or later, and probably in an even more challenging form, as the soul continues on its journey. In any case, whatever the circumstances of one's suffering, whether it concerns a present or past life, the real reason is always the same—resistance to growth.

Earlier in this chapter it was mentioned that by living a Christ-like life, we will not only advance the raising of our own consciousness, but by so doing also participate in the spiritualization of matter and in the freeing of the global Christ consciousness from material limitations. Living the Christ life means making a conscious effort every moment of every day towards realizing the unity of all life, living fully every minute and trying to do one's tasks to the maximum of one's ability. In trying to achieve this one will progressively and automatically acquire the so-called virtues which are usually associated with goodness and the spiritual life. Furthermore, as one approaches the state of unity, one becomes aware of the meaning of the word love.

Love in the sense referred to here, has nothing to do with that syrupy sentimentalism popularized by the movies and romantic literature. The love we mean is a state of consciousness in which one becomes intensely aware of the dynamic unity of all life, and of the attractive and magnetic character of all that is. This state of consciousness has two aspects, which are in fact two sides of one and the same coin. First is the awareness of the oneness of all life, and second is the dynamic aspect of this realization which will oblige us to express this unity in an active way.

It is evident that it would be impossible for a person waking up to the level of consciousness we are considering, to perform acts or even to think thoughts which we generally classify as evil. Would one cut off one's own arm because it did not make the tennis shot which was intended, or would one continuously harbour thoughts of hate and violence against one's leg because one tripped and fell? In the same way, how could one even think of doing harm to one's fellow beings, to animal life or to the physical environment of the planet, if one realizes in a very conscious way that all men and all things form part of a single unity? When realization of this unity becomes generalized it will automatically bring about a different relationship between man and Nature. This new relationship will facilitate a more effective operation of another fundamental law—the law of exchange.

One manifestation of the law of exchange is that if you give something from the heart without expecting anything in return, you will receive something that you really need, possibly from an unexpected source. If man gives love and respect to plants, animals and his physical environment, it is absolutely certain that there will be fewer natural disasters, more reliable and better crops, less need for pesticides and antibiotics. By the same token, if this law of exchange were allowed to operate in the conditions we are discussing, the economic problems which currently threaten the very structure of our society would disappear. There would be no need for economists to wrestle with complicated theories for organizing the production of goods and services. Man would automatically discover how to produce and obtain all he really needs for his physical, social and spiritual well-being.

It is the modern seeker of the Grail, especially those born with the seal of the Temple in their souls, who will have the major responsibility for ensuring the "return" of the Christ. Such people are born with the spiritual capacity to carry out this task. The modern Knight of the Holy Grail does not really need to read books on philosophy, mysticism or occultism to pursue his quest or to serve the cause of the Temple. To live the Christ life the modern Knight does not even have to belong to anything. On the other hand, it would certainly be easier for him to live this life if he joined others working in the same direction. Others will have certain qualities or experience he lacks. In the same way he might be able to give them something they lack. Possibilities for exchange of experience and outlook create a tremendous dynamism which pull all those who have agreed to work together upwards much faster than if they were going it alone. The inspiration and flowering of gifts which such a cooperation can produce has to be experienced to be believed.

A Templar order is but one approach to providing a framework for like-minded individuals to work together and to live the kind of life which the positive forces of evolution so greatly need. A Templar order is more suited to those who have been born, so to speak, with the Temple "in their blood." Such people are marked by destiny or temperament and are the natural pioneers of the age of Aquarius.

It is hoped that this brief account of the meaning of the Cosmic Christ will answer at least some of the questions which modern seekers of the Grail have asked themselves at one time or another. They will surely agree that the approach suggested gives a more hopeful, a lighter and a more joyous dimension to spiritual life, or to life as we live it from day to day. Is it not inspiring to realize that conscious performance of day-to-day duties to the best of one's abilities will bring both spiritual dimensions and material success to our lives? Certainly the concept of the Christ as outlined in these pages must seem more real to us than the rather pious personality we have been lead to believe he was. Is it not fantastic to realize that some vibrations of that Being are in our very cells, waiting to be stimulated into activity? Is it not comforting to contemplate that if these vibrations within us are activated, we will be directly helping to redeem our beloved Mother Earth?

The Virgin and Child, ca. 1340-1350.

CHAPTER IV
THE FEMININE PRINCIPLE

FROM EARLIEST TIMES Man perceived that life around him manifested itself at all levels through a perpetual interplay between the male and female polarities. As he has done with many things, he evolved symbols to represent the male and female principles. The feminine creative principle has been known by many names throughout history. For example, in Babylon it was represented by Ishtar, in Syria Ashtoreth, in Phoenicia Astarte, in Greece Aphrodite, in Egypt Isis, and in the Western world Mary.

The evolution of Mary in the consciousness of the Christian world can be divided into three periods. The first period could be described as the time when the idea of the divine nature of the mother of Christ gradually emerged from her associations with pre-Christian figures such as Isis and Aphrodite. From about 1066, the divine status of Mary became the object of theological scrutiny, followed by controversy until Pope Pius IX put an end to the debate in 1854. From this date onwards the place of the Virgin Mary in the Catholic Church is definitely established.

The name Mary has been interpreted as "myrrh" or "maris" in the sense of bitterness, implying perhaps that like Mary we will all have to undergo purification before the Christ consciousness can be born in us. Mary is sometimes described as *Stella Maris,* Star of the Sea. This is probably to convey the idea of the sea as symbolizing the desire-nature, and the star, the spirit rising above the lower nature. The Virgin Mary is also called the Mater Dolorosa, which translated literally from the Latin means the sorrowing mother, or mother full of grief, as found in the titles of many musical works, the *Stabat Mater Dolorosa.* These works express Mary's agony at the crucifixion and refer to the human aspect of this universal feminine symbol which can understand all sorrows. It is interesting to note in passing that Mary is treated with great respect in Islam—considerable space is devoted to her in the Koran.

Mary is often referred to as *Notre Dame,* a French term meaning "Our Lady" which was used frequently among the Troubadours as a code to hide esoteric teachings on the role of the feminine in spiritual development. St. Bernard of Clairvaux, the spiritual father of the Order of the Knights Templar, was one of those ecclesiastics who realized the importance of the feminine principle not only in the spiritual life of the Church in general, but also for maintaining the psychological balance of his warrior monks. It was not surprising therefore that he placed the Order of the Knights Templar under the protection of Notre Dame. From then on down through the centuries, imposing cathedrals and humble chapels alike have borne witness to the worship of the Eternal Mother.

The Virgin Mary symbolizes three aspects of the feminine principle. The first is that of the Cosmic Mother, which is the female polarity of the Divine. This aspect is sometimes referred to in ancient sacred texts as the Primordial Waters. The second aspect refers to the essence of Mother Earth, which nourishes humanity, her children. The concept of Original Matter is also associated with this aspect. In ancient times, the ancient goddesses Cybele and Demeter were also representations of these ideas. The third aspect of Mary is that of the Mother of God.

In the chapter on the Grail, we have already touched on the importance of finding a balance between the male and female polarities in our lives and in society. Psychoanalysts have stressed the need for today's male-oriented society to give full recognition to the female principle. The old film "The Blue Angel," starring Marlene Dietrich, illustrates in broad terms what happens when the feminine polarity is not allowed to function. In the film, a very respected professor, who has been too busy to pay attention to the creative and emotional sides of himself, one day meets an attractive but unsentimental chorus girl. The girl's exaggerated toughness already gives a clue that she has certain unresolved problems with the male aspect of herself. The professor, unaware of his own particular problem, allows his subconscious to project his repressed femininity onto this attractive "toughie" and proceeds to fall madly in love with her. The girl is amused by the power she holds over this pillar of society and devises all kinds of way to humiliate the poor man. The story, as might be expected, has a tragic ending.

According to the Jungian school of psychoanalysis, many of today's psychological ills are due to the non-integration of our opposite polarities. Followers of Jung have drawn attention to the fact that in the contemporary male the feminine side is repressed, while the opposite is true for the female sex. They also claim that dream analysis can help to reconcile us with the repressed sides of ourselves. Techniques have been employed for centuries by esoteric schools to achieve the integration of the positive and negative polarities of the human psyche. The Temple tradition in particular has been the guardian of many of these techniques.

The Hebrew conception of a masculine creator favored by Moses and the prophets has so strongly influenced the thinking of Western man that even today many people find it difficult to think of God as having feminine characteristics. This state of mind has greatly reinforced the traditional attitude that women are not quite equal to men. Fortunately, as mentioned in the chapters on the Grail, Western society has begun, if as yet unconsciously, to respond to the power of the feminine polarity. The rise of women to positions of power and responsibility hitherto reserved for men is an indication of this evolution.

Because the impact of the feminine polarity on the collective mind of contemporary Western society is not yet being integrated consciously, one can discern a tendency towards overcompensation. As was mentioned above, a similar reaction is produced when an individual has to recognize, accept and express his or her opposite polarity. An example of this phenomenon on the collective level is the current popularity of certain rock and pop stars whose physical appearance suggest either a kind of indeterminate sexual polarity or an image recognizably male, but with strong female overtones. One need not stretch one's imagination to conclude that promoters in the entertainment world have sensed what is happening in the collective unconscious and have tailor-made their performers to act as symbols on which a public reared on masculine values projects its repressed femininity.

Another area where we are witnessing a considerable incursion of feminine influence is in the area of men's fashion. Men's clothes are now available in all colors and materials formerly considered feminine. The word *unisex* is now in use in many countries to describe clothes to be worn by both men and women. This compensatory over-exaggeration of the feminine is certainly temporary as our society edges its way towards a better balance between the masculine and feminine polarities.

It is hoped that this brief introduction to the subject of the feminine archetype will help the reader to realize that the respect rendered by the tradition of the Order of the Temple to "Notre Dame" is not with the intention of worshipping a person, but an attempt to come to terms with and pay homage to one of the most powerful aspects of our Creator.

THE GUARDIANS OF THE TEMPLE TRADITION FROM THE MIDDLE AGES TO OUR TIMES

The dubbing of a Knight.

CHAPTER V
THE KNIGHTS TEMPLAR AND OTHER ORDERS OF CHIVALRY

The Institution of Chivalry

CHIVALRY was a feudal military institution of the nobility. It defined the behaviour of the mounted warrior known as the Knight both on the battlefield and in his social relations with other groups of society such as his equals, his comrades, his enemies, the church, women, the peasantry and the poor. Certain ideals such as nobility of heart, honor, courage, gallantry and generosity have become associated with the notion of chivalry.

The institution of chivalry originated from the mixture of several influences. Germanic military customs were tailor-made for the enormous possibilities opened up by the use of cavalry in the armies of Western Europe in the Middle Ages. Then there was the Church, which sought to limit and control violence by channelling it in certain ways, including the idea that violence could be directed against the enemies of Christendom. Another element was the concept of courtly love popularized by the wandering Troubadours, according to which a noble knight had to develop the finer side of his nature by devoting himself to a lady of his class, and by passing certain tests of character to win her esteem and affection.

Knighthood was first established in France but quickly spread to other Christian countries in Europe. Under the rules of knighthood, an aspirant passed through the ranks of Page, Ecuyer or Squire, and finally to that of Knight. The function of the Page was to personally serve his master and his lady, attend to them during the hunt, and even wait on them at table if the occasion demanded it. The Page was taught love of God, veneration for sacred things, respect for womanhood, and manners and virtues befitting his future status.

The Page was promoted to the rank of Squire in the course of a special ceremony in which a priest blessed the sword and sword-belt which the Squire would carry on his person from that moment on. A Squire could be made a Knight from the age of 21, after having shown proof of fidelity, zeal and valour. The ceremony for admission to the status of Knight was a solemn affair. The future Knight was required among other things to spend several nights praying in a chapel and to undertake a certain amount of fasting. The act by which the aspirant was formally made a Knight was first known as dubbing. Originally it was carried out by administering a blow or a slap to the neck or shoulder, while certain words of welcome or exhortation were uttered. Eventually the practice developed into what was called the accolade, although the word dubbing has persisted into modern times. The accolade involved touching both shoulders of the aspirant with the flat of a sword blade.

A Knight had to embody the virtues he had been taught as a Page and a Squire. He had to be a man of his word and an oath or promise had to be kept no matter what. Lying was a very grave offence and could only be wiped out by the shedding of blood. In short a Knight had to symbolize and inspire all the noble qualities to which a human being could aspire.

The status of knighthood could be conferred at any time, including on the battlefield after some great feat had been accomplished. The most popular occasions, however, were the important religious festivals, especially Pentecost, and during coronations, births and baptisms of kings and princes. The different actions performed during the ceremony of investiture as well as the accoutrements used, were of a symbolic character. The double-edged sword was to remind the newly-dubbed Knight that his task, among other things, was to maintain chivalry and justice. The straight lance symbolized truth, the coat of mail represented a fortress erected against vice, and the spurs were to incite the new Knight to deeds of honour and virtue. The shield was a symbol of his place between the sovereign and his people with the duty to preserve peace.

The Crusades began in 1095 and brought together the Knights of Christendom in a common enterprise under the umbrella of the Church. There began the practice of dubbing Knights at the place believed to have been the burial place of Christ. Knights dubbed at this spot were known as Knights of the Holy Sepulchre. Gradually classes of Knights developed and banded together for some common purpose. Some were fraternities established on religious lines and into which Knights were admitted as monks. Such fraternities followed rules of celibacy and were organized in hierarchical fashion with officials bearing titles such as Grand Master, Grand Prior, Commander and Knight. Some of these orders were international in character, such as the Order of the Knights Templar, the Order of the Hospitallers of St. John of Jerusalem and the Order of St. Lazarus, the last-mentioned devoting itself principally to the protection of leper hospitals. There were also national crusading orders such as the Order of Calatrava in Spain, the Order of Avis in Portugal and the Teutonic Knights in Germany. As these orders grew in wealth and influence, religious aims gave way to political ambitions.

The fading out of the Crusades, the defeat of the Christian armies by the forces of Islam, the development of new military strategies for effectively deploying footsoldiers, the success of bowmen at the battle of Crécy in 1346 and at Agincourt in 1415, the development of artillery and the erosion of feudalism by centralized royal power, gradually destroyed the institution of knighthood. Chivalry degenerated into fashionable elegance and Christian fervor gave way almost completely to courtly love. The old sense of personal honor became egoistic pride to be defended in duels.

With the disappearance of the medieval orders of chivalry, a new type of institution gradually came into being. These were more or less honorary associations established by sovereigns within their respective dominions, and consisting of members whose common link was the possession of the same titular distinctions. Examples of these are the Knights of the Garter, the Knights of St. Andrew and the Knights of the Golden Fleece.

A brief sketch of the history and fortunes of the three main orders of Chivalry is given in Chapters VI to VIII. As the esoteric tradition of the Order of the Temple is the main subject of this book, greater attention will be given to the Order of the Knights Templar.

Jacques de Molay, the last Grand Master of the Order of the Knights Templar.

CHAPTER VI

THE TEMPLARS AND THEIR LEGACY

A Brief History of the Order

IN 1095, Pope Urban II decided to kill two birds with one stone. He would incite the sovereigns of the West to recapture the city of Jerusalem, where the faithful of various religions had managed, though not without difficulty, to tolerate each other's presence since the city fell to the curved swords of Islam in AD 638. The second aim of the Pope was to bring together in the process, by force if necessary, the Eastern and Western strains of Christianity. The military operation through which Urban II hoped to achieve these twin ambitions was termed the First Crusade, an ill-fated enterprise which was to change the course of history.

Pope Urban did not achieve his grand design, but after much bloodletting by Christians and Moslems alike, Jerusalem fell in 1099 to the Christian armies led by Godefroy de Bouillon of Flanders. Ironically, Urban died that same year. In the years that followed anyone wishing to enhance his status felt he had to make a pilgrimage to Jerusalem. In the areas close to the holy sites, Christian soldiers assured the safety of the pilgrims but were unable to do so effectively in certain other places.

Different dates have been given by historians for the founding of the Knights Templar. According to Templar tradition, the founder of the Order, Hugues de Payns, a 48 year old nobleman, and eight other Knights took their vows on 12 June 1118 during a ceremony at the Castle of Arginy, situated about 40 kilometers from Lyons, beside the village of Charentay near Belleville-sur-Saône, in what is today the County of Rhône. The nine Knights formed a brotherhood devoted to Christ, and pledged themselves to ensure the safety of the pilgrims and to the protection of the Holy Sepulchre. Templar tradition holds that the founding knights left that same year for the Holy Land. There is some uncertainty about the exact names of the nine Knights but they are generally believed to have been the following:

Hugues de Payns
Hugues Comte de Champagne
Geoffroy de Saint-Omer
André de Montbard
André de Gondemare
Payen de Montdidier
Archambault de Saint-Aignan
Godefroy Bissor
Roffal

The nine Knights took vows of poverty, chastity and obedience, but also swore to remain fighting men. King Baudouin II of Jerusalem decided to help the Knights, and gave them accommodation in a building very close to the site of the original Temple built by Solomon. The Knights first called themselves the Poor Fellow-soldiers of Jesus Christ, but they later became known as the Poor Soldiers of the Temple of Solomon and then finally assumed their historic title of the Knights Templar.

The next phase in the development of the Order is closely linked to one of the most important personalities of the Middle Ages—Saint Bernard of Clairvaux. No other single person had as much influence on the medieval world as this monk-statesman. Bernard was not only one of the most outstanding men of his time but probably of all time. Any readers unfamiliar with this spiritual giant should seek out the details of his life. They will find it a rewarding experience.

Bernard is described by historians as being a slightly-built man of frail health, constantly bothered by a gastric disorder. Despite these limitations he impressed those who came in contact with him by his iron will, his directness and penetrating mind, his radiant mystical spirituality and his understanding of men and events. These qualities made him the uncrowned master of the medieval world. The great kings of the time sought his advice and friendship.

Bernard was born of a noble family in the Castle of Fontaine near Dijon. In 1112, at the age of 21, he abandoned his riches and presented himself at the monastery of Cîteaux. He quickly persuaded others, including his five brothers, to join him, and very soon they numbered nearly thirty.

Situated about 14 kilometers east of Nuits-St.George, Cîteaux is found in what is today the County of Côte d'Or in France. This region, with its main city Dijon, is famous for its fine Burgundy wines, many of which, like Beaune, Gevrey Chambertin and Aloxe Corton, bear the names of the towns and villages of the region. Except for a few ruins very little of the old monastery remains today.

When Bernard joined the monastery, it was in deep decline. In a short time by energy and example he completely transformed the situation. When he left Cîteaux in 1115, the impulsion he had given to the monastery was so great that three branches were set up, and at the age of only 25 he was named Abbot of the third and now famous monastery of Clairvaux. The village of Clairvaux is about 14 kilometers from the town of Bar-sur-Aube in the County of Aube. The abbey where St. Bernard lived and worked is now used as a prison.

At Clairvaux Bernard and his fellow monks built the first buildings with their own hands on land given to them by none other than a man who was to become one of the founding Knights of the Order of the Knights Templar—Hugues, Comte de Champagne. Within ten years of his appointment as Abbot, Bernard had become one of the most powerful men in the Christian world, mediating in quarrels between the powerful of the land, either putting them in their place or giving them advice and inspiration. Because St. Bernard began his career in Cîteaux, the brand of monastic life he founded has come to be known as the Cistercian Order.

Almost any history book will tell you that Bernard gave encouragement to Hugues de Payns, the man considered to be the founder of the Templars. History books will also tell you that Bernard was involved in one way or another with the drafting of the Rule which was given to the Templars by the Council of Troyes. It is also known that despite illness during the Council, he forced himself to lobby for the ecclesiastical and secular legitimacy of the Order.

Bernard's fame grew and so did that of the Templars. They were given many gifts of land and money by admirers or by those who wished to calm their consciences. In 1125 King Baudouin of Jerusalem gave the title of Master of the Temple to Hugues de Payns. As the Order grew in fame and size, King Baudouin felt that if it could be given official recognition by the Pope, it would be able to help him with his military ambitions. He therefore wrote a letter to Bernard soliciting his help and asked André de Montbard, one of the founding members of the Order and Bernard's uncle, to deliver the letter. Bernard welcomed the initiative and promised to do all he could. Pope Honorius was agreable in principle and convoked a Council to discuss the matter. When he heard the good news, de Payns left immediately for Italy with a number of his Knights where he met the Pope and went on to France to await the opening of the Council which took place on 13 January, 1126 at Troyes.

The Council approved the Rule of the Temple which was to become the new code of conduct for the Knights. The Rule, which covered every aspect of daily life, contained 72 articles. It was extremely strict and severe and was believed to have been inspired by a rule of Essenian origin known as the Rule of the Master of Justice. Great stress was put on obedience, and everything in it was designed to promote communal life among the Knights and to avoid jealousy and pride. The Rule did not cover administrative matters. By 1267 the Knights themselves had added a large number of other articles dealing with the administration of the Order.

The following is a short summary of the structure of the Order which was developed and maintained until the Order's abolition in the 14th century. In order of importance the officers of the Order were:

The Grand Master
The Seneschal
The Marshal
The Commander of the City of Jerusalem
The Commander of the City of Tripoli
The Commander of the City of Antioch
The Provincial Masters in France, England, Aragon, Portugal and Hungary

Other officers were the Draper, the Gonfanonier, and the Turcopolier. Each of the provinces had a hierarchical structure modelled on the headquarters in Jerusalem. The provinces were further divided into Commanderies and Preceptories under Commanders and Preceptors. The Commanderies were sub-divided into "Maisons" or "Houses".

The ranks of the Order were composed of:

Knights
Squires or Ecuyers
Chaplains or Almoners
Sergeants
Tradesmen, masons, craftsmen and artisans
Locally enlisted militiamen called Turcopoles

The Grand Master was the head of the Order. He had very wide powers, but could not take certain decisions without consulting a group of senior Knights known as the Chapter. He had some privileges such as the right to four horses when in the field and to the largest tent, distinguished further from the others by being circular in shape. The Grand Master was always accompanied by the battle standard of the Order, which was known as the Gonfalon Beauceant.

The Seneschal or Commander of the Order was the second in command, and when the Grand Master was absent, it was he who was in full command. The next in the chain of command was the Marshal; he was the supreme military commander. The Commander of the City of Jerusalem was responsible for the general health and well-being of the brothers of the Order as well as the protection of pilgrims. The Commanders of Tripoli and Antioch exercised the authority of the Grand Master in their own territories except when he visited them. The Draper was responsible for clothing, bedding etc. The Gonfanonier was responsible for the instruction of recruits and for the observance of statutes and rules. The Turcopolier was in charge of local cavalry recruits and reported directly to the Grand Master or the Marshal.

The Knights were the main fighting force of the Order. They were assisted by the Squires or Ecuyers. The latter were attached to the Knights as servants while they passed their apprenticeship. The Knights were known for their courage and their oath never to retreat even if the odds were three to one against them. The dress uniform of the Knights was a white cloak bearing a red eight-pointed cross. In battle they wore coats of mail, and their weapons consisted of a mace, a heavy sword, a short lance and a cutlass. The Sergeants, who wore black cloaks, were usually drawn from the bourgeoisie. Because of the importance to the Templars of the artisans in the building trades, they will be described in more detail in Chapter VII in connection with Compagnonage.

The Chaplains were responsible to the Grand Master. Pope Innocent II gave the Templars the right to appoint their own chaplains—under this arrangement they owed allegiance only to Rome and the Grand Master. Innocent II also gave the Templars the right to build their own churches. In fact the situation soon developed whereby the Templars were subject to no authority save that of the Pope. The Order soon became a State within States, a freedom which was to lead to their eventual downfall.

The battle standard of the Knights Templar, the Gonfalon Beauceant or Beauseant, was a red eight-pointed cross on a background of black and white squares. In heraldry, this red cross which had widened ends was known as "Croix pattée gueules." The Beauceant was also known as the Piebald Standard because of the pattern of black and white squares. Scholars of symbolism claim that the white and red colours signify God's wisdom and divine love, while the black and white signify light and darkness, the positive and the negative. According to one source, St. Bernard was supposed to have said that the significance of the black and white background was that the white meant the Templars were good for the friends of Christ, black and terrible for his enemies. There has been much debate as to the origin of the word Beauceant. One story goes that the name came about because one Templar Knight, Gérard de Bouxin, when he saw the standard flying cried out: "Que tu es beau céans!"

The battle cry of the Templars was "A moi, beau sire! Beauceant à la rescousse!" Their rallying cry was "Vive Dieu, Saint Amour!" The device or motto of the Order was a Latin version of the first two lines of Psalm 115, verse 1 *Non nobis, Domine, non nobis, sed Nomini Tuo da gloriam.* This is translated as "Not for us, Lord, not for us, but to Thy Name give glory," signifying that members of the Order lived only for service to the Divine. The seal of the Order sometimes carried a design of two horsemen on the same horse, indicating, *inter alia,* the vow of poverty and the unity which should reign within the Order, as well as the dual role of the Templar as warrior and monk.

To return to the history of the Order, Hugues de Payns travelled through Europe promoting its expansion. He was very successful and obtained gifts of land and property wherever he went. In England and Scotland he also obtained gifts and other forms of support. It is believed that Hugues de Payns visited the famous Temple Church in Chancery Lane, London. The Grand Master left France for the Holy Land in

1129, by which time the Order was solidly established in Europe, including the Iberian Peninsular.

The Order went on to develop rapidly in influence and power. The star of St. Bernard rose with that of the Templars. When Pope Honorius died in 1130, Bernard supported the man who became Innocent II. As a result he had a staunch supporter in the papacy, which as we have seen was of great advantage to the Templars. On 24 May 1136, Hugues de Payns died and was succeeded by Robert de Craon.

On 24 December 1144, Edessa, one of the Christian strongholds in the Holy Land, was recaptured by the Moslems. Bernard canvassed vigorously for a new crusade, and spoke publicly in its support at Vézelay on Easter Sunday, 31 March 1146. In a solemn ceremony in Paris, a new wave of crusaders vowed to avenge this attack on Christendom. Among the great figures present were King Louis II, Pope Eugenius, St. Bernard and three hundred Knights in their new white cloaks with a red cross on the left breast, recently conferred on them by the Pope.

In 1147 the Crusaders left for the Holy Land. The ill-managed and uncoordinated operation turned out to be a catastrophe from start to finish, and the majority of the Crusaders perished, many even before they reached Palestine. The Templars fought bravely but the valor of a few men could not save the day.

This debacle signalled the start of a rough passage in Templar history. The Grand Master died and was replaced by another Frenchman, Evrard de Barre. He resigned after 3 years to become a monk under Bernard de Clairvaux. Bernard himself died on 20 August 1153. Both Pope Eugenius and de Barre followed shortly after. André de Montbard became the fifth Grand Master of the Order, but did not last long, dying on 17 January 1156. On top of all this, the Templars now had to face competition. From the beginning they had been a military order, whereas the Hospitallers of St. John, established a early as 1048, had hitherto essentially been an order devoted to helping pilgrims and the sick. Seeing the great success of the Templars, they decided to organize themselves on military lines and soon began to make their influence felt. In spite of this rivalry, the power of the Templars continued to grow and reached such a point that kings and rulers began to fear and distrust them. In contrast to the Hospitallers, their Rule, their meetings and admission ceremony or "reception" were secret. The fact that the Templars operated in secret and had become international bankers did not endear them to society at large.

The decline of the power of the Knights Templar in the Holy Land resulted from a combination of factors beyond their control. Yet it cannot be denied that the purity and high idealism of the original founders were gradually compromised as circumstances obliged the Templars to be more and more involved in the politics of the Near East. The rank and file of the Order, as well as some of its leaders, did not always maintain the noble ideals present in the early days in the way they lived. Nevertheless, the Templar tradition holds that the inner order retained the high spirituality laid down by Hugues de Payns and his brother Knights right to the end, and this ensured that there was no break in the inner transmission, whatever form this would subsequently take.

In June of 1157 the then Grand Master, Bertrand de Blanquefort, was captured in battle and taken to Damascus in chains. The demise of the Christian presence in the Holy Land had begun. Jerusalem was captured in 1244, and with the fall of St. Jean d'Acre in 1291 to the Mamelouks, the chapter of Christendom's adventure in Palestine was closed.

The Templars and the Hospitallers retreated to Cyprus, after which the Templars went on to Sicily. From there the majority returned to France. The Templars then enjoyed a brief period of peaceful existence, ensconced in their castles and chapels, blissfully unaware, it seemed, that the death knell of the Order had sounded.

In 1304 King Philip IV of France, known as Philip the Fair,

asked to be dubbed a Knight of the Order. Philip was known to be a crafty and scheming sovereign. The Templars no doubt felt that this was probably a move by the King to infiltrate the Order for his own designs, and to Philip's great mortification his request was rejected.

A few years later, one of the King's advisors, Guillaume de Nogaret, suggested to him that one way of replenishing his rapidly dwindling coffers would be to find some way of bringing the Order to its knees and seizing its funds. Philip, remembering how he had been slighted, did not hesitate. On 13 October 1307, the King's soldiers swooped on the Templar strongholds and arrested all Templars who could be located. There followed seven years of trials, forced confessions, retractions, suffering, scandals, falsehoods, pillage and burning at the stake.

On 3 April 1312, during a Council held in the town of Vienne in France, Pope Clément V, accompanied by King Philip, announced the abolition of the Order of the Knights Templar, as a result of a decision taken in private consistory on 22 March of that year. The only concession made was not to pronounce excommunication.

On 18 March 1314, Jacques de Molay, the twenty-second and last Grand Master of the Order, was burnt at the stake on a small island situated on the river Seine in Paris. At the time the island was known as L'Ile des Javiaux; today it is called Place Dauphine. Just before he gave up the ghost, the last Grand Master is said to have cried " . . . woe will come, ere long, to those who condemn us without a cause. God will avenge our death."

Coincidence or not, on 20 April 1314 Pope Clément V died, surrounded only by a few servants who did not hesitate to steal his treasure. On 9 November of the same year, King Philip the Fair was injured while boar hunting near Poissy and died after great suffering on 29 November. Guillaume de Nogaret fared little better; he also died that same year under mysterious circumstances. The prediction of the Grand Master seemed to have succeeded beyond his wildest expectations. The children of Philip the Fair and other members of his immediate family all had short and unhappy lives. Some 14 years after the death of the Grand Master Jacques de Molay, the line of Philip's dynasty disappeared from the throne of France. A French writer, Maurice Druon, has written a number of readable books entitled *Les rois maudits* (The Accursed Kings) on this strange sequence of events. A very successful television series based on his books and performed by members of the Comédie Française was shown in France during the 1960s.

Elsewhere in Europe, the Templars also went into decline, though less rapidly. In the British Isles there was much sympathy for the Templars, and in typically British fashion some sort of a formula was initially worked out whereby the Templars were permitted to keep their property and allowed as private individuals to remain in the Catholic Church. But eventually many of them suffered as their French brothers had done.

In Portugal King Dinis refused to persecute the Templars but avoided a confrontation with the papacy by creating a new order and integrating the Templars into it. In March 1319 Pope John XXII authorized the founding of the Order of Christ, the name given to the new Order. The headquarters of the Order of Christ was established in Tomar in 1356. The last true Grand Master of the Order was Don Lopo Dias de Sousa. After him the sons of the king administered the Order. The first was Prince Henry the Navigator, who became famous for his discoveries. Many Portuguese explorers belonged to the Order and proudly displayed the red cross on the sails of their caravelles. The Order of Christ became a secular order in 1789, and its last chaplains left Tomar in 1834. The Order still exists today but bestows purely honorary titles.

In Spain the tradition of warrior monks found its expression through the Order of the Knights Templar and four national orders: the Orders of Calatrava, Santiago, Alcantara and Montesa. The national orders were not controlled by the international Templar hierarchy. They were however, with the exception of the Order of Santiago, linked with the Cistercian Rule of Cîteaux in one way or another. Santiago was given a Rule directly by Rome.

The Order of Calatrava was the first military order established in Spain. It observed the monastic Rule of Cîteaux and was accepted as an Order in 1164 by Pope Alexander III, but only in November 1187, after much effort by the Spanish, was it confirmed as a Cistercian branch. Like other orders in Spain, the Knights of Calatrava were active in the battles against the Moors. Similarly they were involved in disputes between the different provinces in the country. The last Grant Master of the Order, Don Garcia Lopez de Padilla, died in 1482. The Order was taken over by the crown in 1485, and deteriorated gradually after first limiting membership only to candidates of noble origin and then, in 1540, authorized knights to marry. The remainder of the history of the Order is more or less the history of all the orders in Spain. On 25 July 1835 the Spanish Government suppressed the monasteries. Around the middle of the nineteenth century a Concordat was signed between Rome and the ruling Spanish sovereign which decreed that all the military orders should be grouped in one territory within the province of Ciudad Real. This arrangement was abolished under the Second Republic. In 1939 the orders were allowed to revive but only as purely formal institutions with the right to confer honorary titles.

After the Order of the Knights Templar was abolished, King Jaime II of Aragon resisted the handing over of the property of the military orders to the then Hospitallers. When John XXII succeeded Clément V, he agreed to the solution of creating a new Order in Spain. Thus the Order of Montesa was founded in June 1317, under the first Grand Master Guillen de Eril. A certain number of Knights Templar, as well as those belonging to the national orders, survived by attaching themselves to the new Order. Like the Order of Christ in Portugal, the Order of Montesa was considered to be the legitimate successor of the Temple Tradition and until it was tampered with by royalty, it remained linked to the Cistercian Rule through its close relationship with what survived of the Order of Calatrava.

Certain specialists in the history of the Templars claim they have reason to believe that the secret documents and relics of the Templars were spirited away for safekeeping before they could be seized by Philip the Fair. It is said, for example, that the treasure of the Templars was hidden in the Castle of Arginy by Jacques de Molay's nephew, Philippe, Comte de Beaujeu. Many books have been written advancing various theories as to the hiding places of these treasures. Fortune hunters of all kinds have sought these objects, but so far no one seems to have found them.

As to the question of what happened to the Order in France after the death of Jacques de Molay, the situation has never been clarified. There have been claims that while in prison, de Molay passed on his succession in due form, with orders to perpetuate the Tradition in secret while awaiting friendlier times. This has led to the belief that both Freemasonry and the Rosicrucian tradition were infiltrated early in their history by secret Templars. Those who support this view point to the existence of a degree in Masonry called the Degree of the Knights Templar. In more recent times the mother of the modern Western esoteric tradition—the Order of the Golden Dawn—is also said to have had Templar origins.

One story goes that 237 Knights Templar chaplains and artisans escaped from the France of King Philip IV and took refuge in a Commandery of the Temple in London. Among them was an alchemist named Guidon de Montanor who had reached the higher levels of the art. Montanor adopted one of the escapees, Gaston de la Pierre Phoebus, as his spiritual son, to whom he transmitted the secrets of the Royal Art. After a few months the Templars, or most of them, fearing the greed of Edward, the English king, left for Scotland, probably for the Isle of Mull. There, encouraged by Guidon de Montanor, Gaston de la Pierre Phoebus created a group of alchemists of Templar origin, to whom he communicated the secrets of the Order of the Temple. According to this story, Phoebus formed an occult College composed of himself, de Montanor, Pierre de Lombardie, Richard (an English Templar), Henri de Montfort, César Minvielle, and Pierre-Yorik de Rivault. The college adopted as its symbol the pelican with open wings, feeding its hungry young with its own flesh and blood from an opening in its breast. This is intended to remind us of the Saviour who shed his blood for mankind. The symbol has been adopted by Masonry as the symbol of the eighteenth or Rose Croix Degree of the Ancient and Accepted Scottish Rite. The Masonic interpretation of the symbol is that the pelican, by restoring her young ones to life, symbolizes resurrection.

To continue with the story of the Rose Croix and the Templar tradition, while Phoebus was developing his College, two Popes, Clément V and John XXII, had died. When the persecution of the Templars had completely calmed down Phoebus decided to return to France discreetly with 27 companions. He visited the new Pope, who is said to have been a secret alchemist. The story continues that the Pope asked Phoebus to return to Scotland and to persuade the elite of his brothers-in-arms who were in the service of King Robert the Bruce, to return to France. Knowing that the roads were infested with armed robbers, Phoebus took the precaution of handing over the secret documents of his College at a place called Pont-Saint-Esprit to a former Templar who had become Prior of the Hospitallers of St. John. In the course of his journey Phoebus and 13 of his companions were killed by bandits. He was buried at Pont-de-Gennes, now in the commune of Montfort-le-Rotrou in the region of Sarthe in France.

Five of the survivors reached Scotland to return later to France. They were led by Jacques de Via, nephew of Pope John XXII. The former Templar mentioned above proceeded to draw up a new Templar Rule which was adopted by a College of 33 men. The College elected de Via as successor to Phoebus. All these arrangements were kept secret. On 6 May 1317 Jacques de Via died. His successors have since called themselves "Frères Aînés de la Rose-Croix," in English, the Elder Brothers of the Rose Cross. The story concludes that the tradition still exists today and that the number of members of the College still remains 33, being renewed and maintained by "co-option."

In a book published in France in 1970 by Raymond Bernard, at that time head of the French-speaking branch of the Rosicrucian order AMORC, the author claims that he was asked to reveal the existence of a secret College of men who had reached the level of what is known in esoteric circles as the Rose-Croix. Raymond Bernard describes his visits to some of the secret centers where these Elder Brothers carried out their spiritual activities. According to him, there existed 12 such centers on our planet, and in each there were 12 brothers. No mention was made in Bernard's account of any link with the Phoebus story.

The Twenty-two Grand Masters of the Order of the Knights Templar

1. Hugues de Payns (1118-1136)
2. Robert de Craon
3. Evrard de Barre
4. Bernard de Tremlay
5. André de Montbard
6. Bertrand de Blanquefort
7. Philippe de Milly or de Naplouse
8. Eudes de Saint-Amand
9. Arnaud de la Tour Rouge or de Toroge

10. Gérard de Ridefort
11. Robert de Sablé or de Sabloil
12. Gilbert Erail
13. Philippe du Plessiez
14. Guillaume de Chartres
15. Pierre de Montaigu
16. Armand de Périgord
17. Guillaume de Sonnac
18. Renaud de Vichy or de Vichiers
19. Thomas Béraut or Bérard
20. Guillaume de Beaujeu
21. Thibaut Gaudin
22. Jacques de Molay (1298-1314)

The Legacy of the Templars

The following paragraphs will deal with certain aspects of the real mission of the Templars which relate directly to the purpose of this book, and on which little or no information is given in the usual academic accounts of the history of the Order. As to the veracity of certain assertions, readers will have to accept them on faith, until such time as they can confirm them directly though contact with a genuine Order of the Temple.

One characteristic of the Order of the Temple throughout its different manifestations whether Essenian, Templar or otherwise, is that it appears on the surface of history for a specifically determined period and for a specific mission. It manifests at a precise moment through the chosen temporary institutional vehicle and after the particular spiritual and temporal heritage has been injected, disappears. According to Templar tradition, this is one explanation as to why the Templars, despite their powerful military force, made no resistance to King Philip the Fair. They realized that their mission had been accomplished and that nothing would be served by fighting to retain their power and influence.

The Exoteric and Esoteric Mission of the Templars

The mission of the Knights Templar was two-fold. Firstly, to inject a certain spiritual idealism into the world of their time through a number of concrete actions. Secondly, to ensure the continuity of the Spiritual Tradition of the Temple by seeking out the sacred esoteric heritage of mankind wherever it was to be found, to reunite it, and to present to a certain spiritual elite a synthesis of the Tradition adapted to the Western mentality of the Middle Ages.

Some of their activities were secret, while others were carried out publicly. Some actions, although done openly, had more profound effects on the contemporary world than were apparent. For example, St. Bernard stimulated public awareness of the Feminine Principle by promoting the adoration of the Mother of Christ in the Church, and by encouraging the Templars to dedicate chapels, cathedrals and churches to the Virgin Mary. In the harsh, cruel and male-dominated world of the Middle Ages, the activation of the feminine archetype was extremely important.

The esoteric tradition to which the Templars had access taught them that the universe was conditioned by the laws of sound, colour, number, weight and measure. They knew how to apply these laws so that symbols could be used to develop a closer relationship between man and spiritual realities.

According to the Templar tradition, number was the principle of being on three levels of manifestation, i.e. Divine, Man and Nature. Number in this sense was the expression of the cosmic design and an element of the mysterious harmony which exists in the universe. This vision of things can be traced back to the priests of ancient Egypt and was developed by Pythagoras in the fifth century BC. In the Middle Ages, the science of numbers played an important part in the spiritual research carried out by the Christian mystics, the Jewish Cabalists and the Moslem Sufis.

The numbers 3 and 9 had a particular significance for the

Templars and these numbers were always present in their buildings and churches. The ancients have always deemed the number 3 to be the most sacred of all numbers. According to Plato it was the perfect symbol of the Creator because it contained the properties of the first two numbers. Aristotle added the reflection that 3 contains in itself a beginning, a middle and an end. Gold had strong symbolic meaning for the Templars: to them it symbolized the radiance of the spirit after purification. They therefore associated gold with the number 3, the symbol of the perfect manifestation of unity.

For the Templars the number 3 also symbolized the mystery of the Trinity. Here we find the symbol of the triangle which is 3 as well. The triangle appears in most of the patterns and designs left behind by the Order. The number 3 was always present in the daily life of the Templars: their rite of reception was repeated 3 times; the aspirant had to present himself ritually 3 times; the aspirant took 3 vows; the Templar ate meat 3 times a week; a Knight had 3 horses; he had to accept to fight against odds of 3 to 1, etc.

The number 3 when multiplied by itself gives 9, the number of completion. The number 9 is the only number which when multiplied by any other number always reproduces itself. Like 3 the number 9 has always been considered a sacred number in esoteric tradition. It is not surprising that the founders of the first Templar Order were 9, that the Templars took vows after a waiting period of 9 years, and that the Order was divided into 9 provinces. During their trials they chose 9 members of the Order to defend them, and 9 of them stood before the Council of Vienne when the Order was abolished. Thus the number 9 was with the Templars at the beginning and with them at the end.

The Templars believed that if certain geometrical forms and mathematical relationships were employed in the construction and design of buildings, these would have important spiritual effects on the people who visited them. Sacred buildings such as chapels, cathedrals and churches, were places where man aspired to approach the Divine. It was not surprising that the Templars were particularly interested in church construction and, as we shall see later, this explains their concern for the welfare of the builders and artisans who could erect and decorate buildings according to their specifications. The Templars also made sure that certain symbols were included in the decoration of buildings in order to pass on esoteric knowledge for future generations of initiates. The Templars applied themselves to the business of cathedral building with such industry that over a thousand chapels and churches were constructed with their support in a little under two hundred years.

St. Bernard, the spiritual father of the Order of the Knights Templar, was a passionate believer in the power of specially constructed forms to bring a realization of the Divine to man. He was of course the driving force behind the Templar's monumental building programme which even reflected his tastes in architecture. St. Bernard favoured a rather simple and austere style, probably in reaction to the rich and ostentatious one preferred by the Benedictines of Cluny.

The Templars had negotiated with the Arabs for permission for their church builders to do construction work in the region of Damascus, Jerusalem, St. Jean d'Acre and Cyprus. The Arabs promised not to molest them so long as they did not bear arms. The builders were placed under the general authority of a Knight named Guy de Lusignan. These builders, known as Compagnons, were men who had spent many years experimenting in order to develop what later became known as Gothic architecture. In their day-to-day tasks the builders owed obedience to de Lusignan but in their spiritual life they owed allegiance to the Templars.

According to Raoul Vergez, a Frenchman and modern Compagnon, some time around 1145 the Templars and the leaders of the Compagnons formalized the Rule known as the "Saint Devoir" or the Rule of the Holy Duty, which governed the manner and spirit in which the latter practised the art of construction, and established the relationship between Templars and Compagnons. Under this arrangement the Templars committed themselves to protect the Compagnons, while the latter agreed to place their skills at the disposal of the Templars. There was probably also an undertaking by the Compagnons to keep secret such teachings about the esoteric aspects of construction as the Templars would pass on to them.

This was a good arrangement for the Compagnons—without the protection of the Templars, they would have been obliged to place themselves under vassalage to some ruler who would not particularly respect their customs. (These included the traditional working journey around France which every builder had to perform before he was recognized as a Compagnon). Under the Templars they enjoyed a better status than the serfs and could travel freely under Templar protection.

In a way, the Compagnons du Saint Devoir were the first organized movement in the world of the working man. During the period of Templar ascendancy, there were also other craftsmen and artisans who did not belong to the Saint Devoir, but wishing to escape from the rigid structure of their feudal lords, pledged oaths of vassalage to the Templars.

One of the techniques which the Compagnons learned from the Templars was the art of choosing the place where a church should be located. The fathers of the Church had long suspected that certain earth currents were useful in enabling contact to be made with cosmic currents, and that the junction of these two types of forces created conditions which were propitious to prayer and mystical contemplation. There is a story that this knowledge was acquired by the Church from a man called Stanislas, who had inherited a family gift which enabled him to identify telluric currents. It is said that Stanislas established that sacred buildings should always be placed so that they could benefit from telluric or earth currents which flow from north to south. It seems that it is also helpful to place a church altar above an underground stream.

The Compagnons developed a particular approach to their trade. Their art was dedicated not just to the creation of beautiful buildings, but to the construction of forms which were also functional, by glorifying the Creator and forging a living link with Him. The trade of constructing sacred buildings was initiatic in the sense that the master builders kept secret their art and passed on their secret skills only by word of mouth. Certain instructions, especially those associated with the application of spiritual laws in the craft, were transmitted only after the apprentice had passed certain ordeals to test aspects of his character. It was these master builders, the Compagnons, inspired by their Templar masters, who worked certain hermetic keys into the geometry and forms they created to decorate cathedrals and churches.

The island of Cyprus has important associations with the Compagnons. It was here that the results of their research into building techniques were first tested. In 1195 Guy de Lusignan was recognized as King of Cyprus. It was natural that because of his earlier associations with these master builders of the Saint Devoir he became their champion on the island. He actively helped those who had survived expulsion from the Holy Land or could not make a living in France. It was here in Cyprus under the protection of de Lusignan that the followers of the Saint Devoir probably lived their most exciting days in an atmosphere where manual work was elevated by spiritual discipline and Templar ideals of chivalry. Unfortunately, with the exception of a few esoteric circles, the influence of Compagnonage in the spiritual odyssey of Western civilisation has virtually disappeared.

The Strands of the Tradition

St. Bernard of Clairvaux considered it his personal mission to reunite the different strands of the spiritual tradition and to adapt this synthesis to the age in which he lived. He had access not only to teachings known to the early Church fathers but, through family connexions, he had also been trained in Druidic lore. He despatched his Knights Templar on secret missions to seek teachings which had been guarded for centuries in certain brotherhoods of the Islamic and Judeo-Egyptian traditions.

The nine Knights sent by him to Jerusalem could not seriously have been sent just to guard the pilgrims. What could such a small body of men achieve as a police force in hostile territory? The real task of the nine Knights in Jerusalem was to carry out research in the area in order to obtain certain relics and manuscripts which contained the essence of the secret traditions of Judaism and ancient Egypt, some of which probably went back to before the days of Moses.

There is no doubt that the nine founding Knights fulfilled this particular mission and that the knowledge obtained from their finds was taught in the oral tradition of the Order of the Temple's secret circles. Hence the rumors that when the Templars were seized by King Philip certain relics were spirited away for safe keeping.

The Templars are said to have had close contacts with the Troubadours, those wandering minstrels whose poetry and song entertained the courts and peoples of Europe with stories of noble deeds. Some of these were themselves secret Templars, as is said of Wolfram von Eschenbach, the man who popularized the Grail legends. One of these legends relates that Gamuret, a knight and father of Parsifal, had another son named Feirefiz by a Moslem woman. Feirefiz also reaches the Castle of the Grail but cannot see the Grail itself until he is baptized, to which he agrees in order to marry the Grail King's daughter, whom he loves. Feirefiz is then able to contemplate the Grail, around which appears a message advocating tolerance for other races and creeds. The marriage takes place and a son is born, the legendary Prester John, future guardian of the Grail.

There were links between well known alchemists and the Templars. One of these was Raymond Lull, a respected Catalan monk born in 1232. Lull, as well as being an alchemist, was a member of a secret circle of the Order of the Knights Templar. It is known that Lull was present as an influential member of the Church at the abolition of the Order at the famous Council of Vienne. Lull did not attempt to intervene. Either he was privy to knowledge that the Order had arrived at the end of its cycle or he had simply concluded that there was no more he could do to influence events. He had argued strenuously for the unification of the Templar and Hospitaller Orders in the hope of thus saving the Templars, but in vain—Grand Master Jacques de Molay remained firmly opposed to the merger.

Links have also been traced between the Templars and Cabalism, the esoteric branch of Judaism. Several writers have alluded to the contacts which existed between the Templar tradition in Spain and the famous Cabalistic schools of the Iberian peninsula.

The Secret Missions of the Templars

In addition to activities related above, the Templars were entrusted with a number of secret missions. One of these was to work for the linking of Christianity and Islam.

The word Islam means "confident submission to God." Islam is the religion promulgated by the Prophet Mohammed, and someone who accepts Islam is a Moslem. Islam dates from the seventh century AD when Mohammed, a well-to-do Arab merchant, received instructions in a vision to bring the message of the One God to the Arab world. Mohammed himself did not claim to have started a new religion, but is reported to have said that his task was merely to bring to his countrymen the message of monotheism already declared by the patriarch Abraham and other prophets such as Moses and Jesus.

There is documentary evidence that despite the continuous state of military confrontation which existed between the Christian and Moslem armies in the Holy Land, there were very close contacts between the Templars and certain Moslem brotherhoods. It is known that the Templars signed secret treaties with the Islamic sect of the Ismailis, and it was demonstrated on several occasions during combat between Arab and Templar forces that certain ideals of chivalry were respected on both sides.

There were of course the famous contacts between the Templars and the Fraternity of the Assassins, a secret fraternity and offshoot of the Ismailis founded around 1090 by Hassan Sabah. The head of the Fraternity was known as Sheikh-el-Jebel, or "the Old Man of the Mountains." Certain historians have argued that the real meaning of the title was "the wise man or sage of the Cabala or Tradition."

Although opinions differ as to the real nature of the Assassins, there is general agreement that the Fraternity taught a secret doctrine which was transmitted only to the initiated. There must certainly have been some connexion between the Assassins and Sufism. It also appears that the organization of the Fraternity and its religious codes and regulations greatly resembled those of the Templars.

The old belief that the Assassins were a fraternity of drugged murderers (the Arabic word *hashishin* meaning partaker of "hashish," the local marijuana) may have been greatly exaggerated during the period of the Crusades when anything pertaining to Islam was given an unsavoury reputation in Western Europe. Unfortunately the word assassin was adopted in some European languages with the meaning it has today, although it may well have derived from the Arabic word "assas," meaning foundation.

A brief digression concerning the fraternity known as the Druze might be in order here. This group is found in Lebanon, Syria and Israel today. Certain authors have suggested that some of the teachings of the Druze might be of

Templar origin, and members of the fraternity do talk of their co-religionists in Europe, especially in Scotland! Contacts between the sect and the Knights Templar could easily have occurred during the period of Templar presence in the Holy Land, although this view may have arisen because Druze teachings are a mixture of Judaism, Christianity and Islam, and include elements of Gnosticism. Within this amalgam is a secret oral tradition said to be practised by an inner group whose initiates are known as Akkals or Okkals, and who possess seven secret books of teachings accessible until recently only to the "pure". Four volumes believed to contain these books have now been published in Arabic, not long after Druze villages in Lebanon were taken over by Phalangist Christians. No denial of the books' authenticity has been issued by the Druze sect, an omission which is significant in itself.

It is also believed that there were contacts with those Moslems who had settled as conquerors in Spain. Although there is no direct relationship to the story of the Templars, it is nevertheless interesting to note that the man considered to be the greatest mystic in the history of Islam, Ibn Al 'Arabi, was born in Murcia, Andalucia. He first studied law in Seville, moved to the Middle East where he was initiated into Sufism in 1194, and died in Damascus in 1240 after an extraordinary spiritual career.

The flowering of the Sufi tradition was also conterminous with the rise of the Templars. Although Sufism had already existed from the early phases of Islam, it was only around the tenth or eleventh century AD that it was institutionalized. The most important Sufi brotherhoods were founded between the twelfth and fourteenth centuries, but the golden age of Sufism was the twelfth century. It is therefore probable that given their mission the Templars would have been busy obtaining information during this period of spiritual ferment in Islam.

Mention was made in Chapter I of the transmission of the

Tradition to Abraham by Melchisedek. This heritage was subsequently diverted into the three main currents of Christianity, Islam and Judaism. It was the task of St. Bernard and the Templars to try to bring them together again.

The Templars did not succeed in outwardly reuniting these currents. They did however manage to maintain the contact with Islam and to integrate certain teachings, as mentioned above. Through the Essenes and the Cabalists elements were also transplanted from Judaism, all of which were to vitalize the spirituality of the Western peoples for the centuries which followed.

Another secret mission of the Templars was to strive for the Return of the Christ. Their terminology for this objective was the "Return of the Christ in Solar Glory." This is the priority mission of the Temple today, and has already been discussed in Chapter III. One additional point can be more appropriately made here. It concerns the puzzlement of historians as to why the Templars, with all their wealth and power, so meekly and passively accepted the destruction of the Order by Philip the Fair. The Templar tradition indicates that the main officers of the Order believed that one day the Order, like the Christ, would have to sacrifice itself physically in order to facilitate the return of the Christ *in victu*. This could explain their courage in battle and why many of them accepted death and the decline of their Order during the period of the persecutions without physically defending themselves.

Times have changed. In the present cycle, the modern Templar will not be expected to sacrifice himself at the stake as did Grand Master Jacques de Molay that cold October day in 1314. The Templar of today will rather be expected to sacrifice the selfish aspects of his nature so that the spirit of the Universal Christ shall manifest in him *in victu*. To describe this in alchemical language: man needs to master the cross of the four elements in order to achieve the awakening of Cosmic Unity and Consciousness in his being. The four elements are symbolized in alchemy by the equilateral cross. Each of the four alchemical elements is ascribed to an arm of the equilateral cross and coincides with one of the four cardinal points of the compass. Each of the elements represents among other things an aspect or quality in ourselves which, if out of balance with the other three elements, brings the negative aspects of that element into our life and behavior. Below are given some examples of the positive and negative qualities of the different elements.

ELEMENT OF EARTH

Positive qualities	Negative qualities
Punctuality	Unreliability
Firmness	Stubbornness
Confidence	Selfishness

ELEMENT OF AIR

Positive qualities	Negative qualities
Cheerfulness	Quarrelsomeness
Diligence	Fickleness
Kindness	Tendency to gossip

ELEMENT OF FIRE

Positive qualities	Negative qualities
Activity	Irritability
Keenness	Bossiness
Resolution	Intolerance

ELEMENT OF WATER

Positive qualities	Negative qualities
Modesty	Timidity
Docility	Passivity
Intuition	Credulity

In alchemy and certain other esoteric traditions such as the Cabala, symbols have been evolved to represent each of the four elements. There are ways known to initiates by which these symbols can be manipulated through meditation or other techniques to bring about a balance of the elements in the practitioner, so that within him negative qualities can be neutralized and balanced by positive qualities. In simple terms, when an individual manages to master the unbalanced or warring elements in himself by working on his character, his weaknesses and uncontrolled impulses, he will have sacrificed his ego and will no longer be tied to the cross of the elements. He will become free from unbridled domination, thus enabling the Christ within to manifest. The alchemist would say that such a person had managed to purify the dross or impurities in his metals through the force of sacrifice and self-discipline, transmuting these metals into the alchemical gold of an awakened spiritual awareness.

The Coming of the Paraclete

Yet another secret mission of the Templars was to prepare the coming of the Paraclete. The original texts of the New Testament were written in Greek. In the Greek text of the book of St. John, the word *Parakletos* appears several times in Chapters XIV-XVI. This word has been translated into English as "Comforter." No single English word, however, conveys all the significance of the Greek *Parakletos* which has meanings relating to defender, helper, comforter and advocate. Some theologians therefore prefer to use the anglicized word Paraclete.

At the Last Supper, after the Christ had revealed to his disciples that he would be betrayed and would not be with them physically for very long, he told them that he would be followed by the Paraclete, a manifestation of the Holy Spirit or the Spirit of Truth. Christ went on to give a number of hints about the nature of the Paraclete. He indicated six characteristics or functions:

1. It would be with the disciples, and in them (John 14, 17).
2. It would teach and recall the teachings of Christ (John 14, 26).
3. It would testify of the Christ (John 15, 26).
4. It would make men aware of their errors, and of what is really meant by justice (John 16, 8).
5. It would guide men into an authentic realization of what is truth (John 16, 13).
6. It would prophesy (John 16, 13).

The Templars considered the Paraclete to be the manifestation of the Holy Spirit as the Spirit of Truth and Revelation. For them its coming would herald the completion of the cycle of a phase in the evolution of our planet, when the Triune nature of the Divine will have been brought in through concrete manifestation—the Father aspect through Melchisedek, the Son aspect through the Christ manifested in Jesus of Nazareth, and the aspect of the Holy Spirit through the Paraclete. The Templars believed that they were given the mission of preparing men's minds for the coming of the Paraclete, so that one day they would be able to perceive truth directly without the intermediary of a spiritual teacher or master. Today it is believed that we have now entered the Age of the Paraclete. Accordingly, men and women in our time will need to make less efforts to develop their spiritual intuition than their forbears in earlier cycles. The coinciding presence of the Paraclete and the currents of the Aquarian Age will ensure that our current cycle will be unique in the history of our planet.

Returning to the particular attributes of the Paraclete, the Cosmic vibrations which work through the aspect of the Divine which is called the Holy Spirit have begun to manifest. Not only will they accelerate the development of man's spiritual intuition if he makes the necessary efforts to purify his vehicles by living the Christ life, but the power of the Paraclete will dynamize the uncovering of truth in all areas of life. Already one can observe that many former secrets are being forced into the open, and the general public is becoming rapidly aware of many things, both spiritual and material, which have been hidden for centuries.

The modern Templar, like his predecessor in the Middle Ages, has a special responsibility to facilitate the unfolding of the Paraclete and to propagate the awareness of the new influences by the state of spirituality he radiates. He will not need to go about enquiring into hidden things. By his efforts to purify himself and to open himself to the new influences he will automatically stimulate the realization of what truth is in the people around him. The law of cause and effect (or Karma) will guarantee that Templars of today will reap the harvest of seeds sown by the martyred warriors of the red cross some six hundred years ago.

The Christ force, now accelerating the return to its Source, is facilitating the entry onto the scene of the Holy Spirit or Paraclete, which has the particular role of awakening in Man the realization of Truth. In turn the action of the Paraclete will favor efforts by the Christ Consciousness to free itself from the restriction of matter. If man plays his part, the action and reaction of these two positive forces will ensure that the program for the return of Cosmic Consciousness back to the Divine Creator, in the sense we have mentioned in this book, will be carried out on schedule. The French translation of the Greek word *Parakletos* as "Consolateur" with the etymological meaning of "he who restores together" sums up this process well. It suggests the coming together of the Godhead and its physical creation.

CHAPTER VII

THE KNIGHTS OF MALTA AND THE TEUTONIC KNIGHTS

The Knights of Malta

AT DIFFERENT TIMES in their history, the Knights of Malta have been variously known as the Knights Hospitallers, Knights of St.John of Jerusalem, and the Knights of Rhodes. This order was one of the most important of the religious orders which came into existence during the Crusades. It began as the Hospitallers of Jerusalem, a wholly religious and charitable Order, established by Italian merchants in Palestine to help poor pilgrims.

In the year 1099, Gérard, Rector of the Hospital and a Frenchman from Martigues in Provence, induced the brethren to take vows of poverty, obedience and chastity. The Patriarch of Jerusalem granted them the habit of the Order, a plain black robe with a white eight-pointed cross on the left breast. Around 1120 Gérard died and was succeeded by Raymond du Puy, who changed the character of the Order by making it into a military one. He wished it to be active in the field and to devote itself to the protection of Palestine from the "infidels." The constitution of the Order along military lines by du Puy is considered to be the beginning of the Order of the Knights Hospitallers of St. John. According to some sources, however, the Order was constituted as early as 1113 when Pope Pascal II was said to have issued a Bull authorizing its establishment.

From about 1120 onwards until the middle of the sixteenth century the history of the Order was one of continuous warfare with the armies of Islam. When the Order, along with other defenders of Christendom, was expelled from the Holy Land, it took refuge in Cyprus. The knights were not happy there, and after seizing the island of Rhodes settled on that island for some two hundred years, during which they acted as an outpost against the encroachment of Ottoman power. In the meantime their rivals, the Knights Templar, were crushed and some of their possessions and properties given to the Hospitallers.

In 1522 the Turks captured Rhodes, and after finding temporary refuge in Italy, the Order was granted the island of Malta by the Emperor Charles V of Germany. In 1530 the Knights of St. John took possession of Malta, where they were to remain for 268 years until it was given up without a struggle by Grand Master Ferdinand von Hompesch in 1798. The Order has nevertheless managed to survive into modern times, existing today mainly as a charitable institution.

The Order of the Teutonic Knights

During the Crusades, a wealthy German living in Jerusalem built a hospital to take care of pilgrims from his country. The Patriarch of Jerusalem gave him permission to add an oratory to the hospital. Other Germans from the towns of Lubeck and Bremen contributed to the development of this charity and for the building of a hospital in Acre. In 1190 Pope Clément III approved the creation of the Order of Teutonic Knights and in 1196 Pope Celestin III granted it the same privileges as other orders.

Heinrich Walpot was elected the first Grand Master. The knights of the order adopted as dress a white mantle with a black cross embroidered in gold. Later a black double-headed eagle was added. After the fall of Acre, the main body of the Knights returned to Europe where for many years they engaged in crusades against the pagan inhabitants of Prussia and Poland, progressively losing their religious character in the process. After accumulating great power in Eastern

Europe the Order went into decline for a variety of reasons, including the loss of its religious fervor. The little which survived of the Order was taken over by the Emperor Francis II between 1805 and 1809, in which year it was abolished by Napoleon.

CHAPTER VIII

ORDERS OF CHIVALRY IN MODERN TIMES

THE MODERN DESCENDANTS of the orders of chivalry have been unkindly described by their detractors as being either mild, benevolent charitable institutions, or mutual aid societies composed of people who enjoy titles and dressing up. Those who have taken it upon themselves to defend these orders claim that some of them have an esoteric side dedicated to the spiritual development of an elite who work quietly and without fanfare for the evolution of humanity. To their credit, the still-active traditional orders have remained discreet in the face of assertions made both by their detractors and their defenders.

The Order of the Knights of Malta, after many vicissitudes, exists today with headquarters in Rome. Sometime after his expulsion from Malta by Napoleon, von Hompesch abdicated his position as Grand Master in favor of the Russian Tsar Paul I, and subsequently died in poverty in Montpellier, France, in 1803. After his abdication there followed a period of confusion during which the post of Grand Master was abolished.

In 1803 Pope Pius VII appointed Jean Tommasi as head of the Order. Throughout the nineteenth century the Knights of the Order pressed continually but without success to be given back the island of Malta. The headquarters of the Order was established in Rome in 1834 after the Russian Commanders of the Order were persuaded to give up their claims to primacy. During the period which followed there were continuous difficulties with the Papacy. These were settled in 1961 when the Order also adopted a new constitution.

Today the Order of the Knights of Malta comprises some 9,000 members throughout the world. The activities of the Order are now essentially charitable and humanitarian. The Order has diplomatic relations with some 42 countries, mostly in Western Europe and Latin America (with the exception of the United Kingdom and the Scandinavian countries).

Apart from a number of ecclesiastics, the membership of the Order is divided into three classes. Members of the first are known as Knights of Justice. These are members who have taken vows of obedience, poverty and chastity, accepted particular rules and are subject to Canon law. The second category are called Knights of Obedience. These are those who have formally undertaken to follow a Christian life according to the spirit of the Order. Finally there are those who have not given a formal undertaking but who have agreed to live a Christian life and to participate in the humanitarian activities of the Order.

Contrary to the Order of the Knights Templar, the Order of the Knights of Malta has never admitted to any esoteric activities. However, it is believed that at least one of the Grand Masters of the Knights of Malta, Manuel Pinto de Fonseca, was a high initiate of the Temple. The story goes that it was Pinto who initiated the famous Count Cagliostro into the Tradition of the Temple.

As far as the Teutonic Knights are concerned, in 1809 Napoleon abolished the Order in all the countries of the Rhine Confederation. The Order continued however in Austria and its headquarters were transferred to Vienna. In 1839 the old Rule of the Order was updated. In 1840 communal living was established among the clergy and a female branch instituted. After a papal decision in 1929, the Order dropped its links with chivalry and returned to its original aims of promoting charitable activities largely in Austria, South

Tyrol, West Germany and Yugoslavia. In 1938 the National Socialist government abolished the Order. It was reinstated after the second World War, and now continues modestly in Germany as a religious community devoted to charity, teaching and good works.

As mentioned previously, towards the end of the Middle Ages kings and princes had begun the practice of creating secular orders with the purpose of forming elite groups bound to the royal person. These orders had nothing in common with the old institution of chivalry except for titles, the act of dubbing and the awarding of insignias. A few of these honorary orders have survived into modern times.

In some countries, particularly the United States of America, there are many fraternal organizations of a social, benevolent character which describe themselves as orders of knighthood, but which do not have or claim to have links with the tradition of chivalry.

As far as the Order of the Knights Templar is concerned, from time to time various orders have sprung up, especially in France, all claiming direct lineage from the original Order founded by Hugues de Payns. Today in France there are all kinds of orders, some pure in intention, some less so, and others quite ridiculous in their pretensions. Not infrequently, many of these orders, instead of getting on with the job in hand, spend a great deal of time and energy deriding other orders whom they consider to have a lesser claim to legitimacy. It is not the purpose of the writer to discredit any particular order. He believes in the old biblical admonition, "By their fruits ye shall know them."

That being said, the choice of a Templar order today is not an easy one. No matter which order is chosen one is bound to hear tales originating in other orders of some kind of unethical behavior by those in charge of the order of one's choice. There are some orders in which the officers in charge are administratively and intellectually capable, but lack the spiritual radiation which can transform the spiritual lives of members in concrete ways. There are others whose leaders are honorable but continue to adhere rigidly to procedures and practices drawn up for the Middle Ages. In this kind of situation what often happens is that dynamic members continuously leave, taking whatever little spirit there is, leaving the letter and the form to a few moribund chiefs who would probably die of shock if anything else happened. There are also situations where orders are run by individuals whose personal lives do not seem to correspond to the lofty ideals they preach. Sometimes a very capable and inspired leader arrives on the scene and is given control by a grateful membership only to find that he and the order are never allowed by other orders to live down the misdeeds or shortcomings of his predecessor.

Against this background the picture for aspirants, particularly in continental Europe, where orders abound, might not seem a very inspiring one. In practice the situation is not as bad as it appears. One thing the aspirant should realize is that one of the first tests he will encounter on the path to spiritual development is that of discernment or discrimination.

In the English-speaking world, where there are few if any operative Templar orders, the situation is much easier. The main reason for the scarcity of Templar orders has quite simply been the question of language. Nearly all existing Templar orders originate in France. Even where branches exist in countries outside France, the senior members of the local branches must be able to communicate with headquarters in French. Although in some ways this has been a blessing, in the sense that non-European seekers have been largely spared the growing pains of the Templar revival, it is at the same time a pity that the immense body of spiritual knowledge available to the Templar Tradition is not yet accessible to the English-speaking (and other) regions of the world. One of the purposes of this brief introduction to the Temple Tradition is to stimulate others to fill this gap.

THE ESOTERIC TRADITION AND THE TEMPLE

In the following chapters the writer will give a brief summary covering those contributions which he feels have had a predominant influence on the Western Tradition. It follows that there are many other groups, movements and individuals both in the past as well as in modern times which have not been mentioned but which have also played their roles in adding to our experience of humanity's long quest for the Grail. To cite one, the activities of the Theosophical Society have not been mentioned since in the view of the writer the Society's inspiration more properly belongs to the Oriental Tradition.

It will be seen that some of the strands we have examined have co-existed with the Templars, and from all indications have contributed to the spiritual knowledge gathered by that Order. In turn, a number of the strands have themselves been directly or indirectly enriched by the Order.

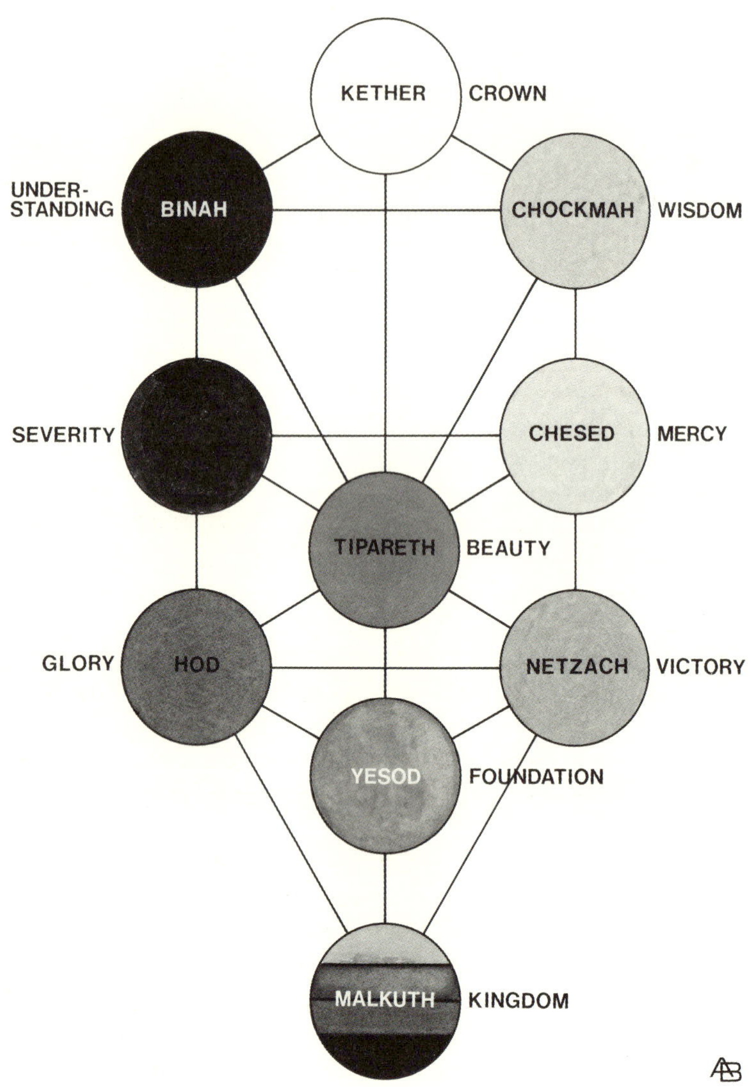
KETHER
CROWN
UNDER-
STANDING
BINAH
CHOCKMAH
WISDOM
SEVERITY
CHESED
MERCY
TIPARETH
BEAUTY
GLORY
HOD
NETZACH
VICTORY
YESOD
FOUNDATION
MALKUTH
KINGDOM
AB

CHAPTER IX
THE CABALISTS

THE WORD CABALA, also written Qabbala or Kabbalah, is of Hebrew origin. It has been translated as "to receive" but means literally "the tradition." As the combination of these two ideas suggests, the Cabala has been essentially an oral tradition within which the secrets of Jewish mysticism are passed on through initiation into teachings and practice under a guide experienced in the system. The Cabala is described as a tradition in the sense that it claims to represent the esoteric part of the oral Torah revealed to Moses. In fact Cabalism includes the entire range of esoteric doctrine and practice which had arisen during the first and second centuries of the Christian era and developed particularly from AD 1200 onwards.

In the period between the third and sixth centuries, a work appeared which came to be known as the *Sepher Yetzirah* or *Book of Creation*. This is the earliest text of speculative Jewish mysticism, and it describes the process of creation in terms of 10 primordial emanations called *Sephiroth*. The work links the 22 letters of the Hebrew alphabet to the 10 *Sephiroth* to form symbolic keys to a comprehensive philosophical system called the 32 Secret Paths of Wisdom.

Dissatisfied with the traditional interpretation of Judaism, certain Cabalists rebelled against the excessive rationalism of the Jewish philosophers. They began to create a new dimension of religious experience in the thirteenth century. This was a decisive period in the development of the Cabala and was due to the work of the Jewish mystics of Provence in France during the second half of the twelfth century, and in Spain, especially in the region of Gerona, during the first half of the thirteenth century.

In the last quarter of the thirteenth century, the many strands of Cabalism merged in a work which made its appearance under the title *Zohar* or *Book of Splendor*. The exact origin of the book is obscure, and there is controversy as to whether it was the rediscovered work of Simeon ben Yohai, a famous second century teacher, or a fourteenth century compilation by Moses de León from Guadalajara in Spain.

In the fourteenth century Joseph Gikatila wrote *The Gates of Light,* which further developed the doctrine of the *Zohar* by linking the Divine Names of God to the individual *Sephiroth*. The expulsion of the Jews from Spain in 1492 led to a revival of interest in the mysticism of the Cabala. This revival was concentrated in the little town of Safed situated in Upper Galilee in that part of Palestine which is now Israel. Some of the famous names associated with this revival were those of Moses Cordovero and Isaac Luria. The last-mentioned made an important contribution to Cabalistic philosophy. His influence was very strong in seventeenth and eighteenth century Jewish history, and he is considered to have indirectly prepared the ground for that popular form of Jewish mysticism which developed among eighteenth century Jews of Eastern Europe known as Hasidism.

Since the last half of the nineteenth century, Cabalistic teachings, especially the practical aspects, were modernized by a number of practitioners, including W. Wynn Westcott and S.L. MacGregor Mathers in the late 1800s, and Arthur Edward Waite, Aleister Crowley, Dion Fortune (Violet Firth), and Israel Regardie in the early part of this century. In the 1960s, W.A. Butler continued the work of his modern predecessors of adapting and popularizing the Cabala. Some contemporary practitioners continue this work, notably Gareth Knight, W.E. Gray and Z'ev Ben Shimon Halevi.

According to Cabalists, the Supreme Being, which is an absolute and inscrutable Unity, contains all within Him. This Unity is *Ain Soph*, meaning the Infinite One, the inherent creative principle. Such a lofty being, according to the Cabalists, could not create directly since it had no finite qualities. It therefore created indirectly by means of a series of 10 spheres from within the Infinite Light itself. These 10 emanations are called *Sephiroth* or Splendors of the Infinite One. The creative principle descends from *Kether*, the first created *Sephirah* (singular of Sephiroth), following a serpent-like path down through a series of Sephiroth arranged in triads. Each *Sephirah* manifests progressive states of destiny until the lowest *Sephirah, Malkuth* or physical life, is reached.

The disposition of the 10 *Sephiroth* in a particular pattern linked by 22 paths is called *Otz Chiim* or the Tree of Life. According to the Cabalists the same arrangement exists in miniature within man's psycho-spiritual organism.

Historical accounts of the development of Cabalism have now given much information on what is generally called the Practical Cabala. In the beginning, this aspect was kept secret and only transmitted orally, but over the centuries information on practical Cabalistic techniques was gradually leaked, and when the secret teachings of the Order of the Golden Dawn (see Chapter XV) were published in the late 1930s, the practical Cabala became public knowledge.

In brief, the practical Cabala teaches that the 10 spheres or *Sephiroth* and the 22 connecting paths, which together form the Tree of Life, are a symbolic system of relationships which can be manipulated either subjectively or objectively using certain techniques. For example, using the tree subjectively, one can, by dynamizing and manipulating the corresponding centers within oneself, become in resonance or harmony with the forces of the Cosmos, i.e. with the different aspects of God symbolized by the different *Sephiroth*. This would bring about a process of psycho-spiritual integration or illumination.

The Cabalists teach that the Tree can also be used objectively. By this they mean that initiates of the system can, through the use of rituals based on Cabalistic symbols and relationships, manipulate cosmic forces which can also affect the external life of the practitioner, including persons and events. Of course they also teach that if the powers obtained in this way are not used altruistically, Nature will exact drastic payment for the selfish abuse of such forces.

It is certain that the Knights Templar obtained access to Cabalistic teachings. As was the case with Islamic Sufism, the rise of the Templars coincided with the development of Judaic Cabalism. The spiritual esotericism of both Islam and Judaism were united with that of Christianity through the Templars, who were the *de facto* spiritual heirs of the early Church Fathers.

CHAPTER X
THE ALCHEMISTS

THE WORD ALCHEMY is derived from a combination of Arabic and Greek words. It originally meant the "Egyptian Art." This relates to processes which, it is believed, were used by the Egyptians to transform the nature of certain metals. In antiquity, Egypt was called "Al Kemit" or the black one. Alchemy was said to have been first taught in Egypt by Hermes Trismegistus, a legendary Egyptian legislator, priest and philosopher who supposedly lived in the reign of Ninus about 2000 BC. So closely has legend associated Hermes with alchemy that the latter also became known as the Hermetic Art. The legacy of Hermes was in fact the teaching of Egyptian and Greek initiates belonging to esoteric circles in and around Alexandria. These initiates found it convenient to use terms and language employed by metallurgists and certain other artisans of the time in order to keep their teaching and mystical experiences secret. One such set of writings which has come down to us from antiquity is said to have been written by Hermes himself on an emerald tablet. Included in this text was the famous axiom of Hermes "As above, so below."

During the early part of the Christian era the Neo-Platonists became interested in the subject and introduced it as a new science—it was at about this time that people began to call it alchemy. Around the eighth century, the Moslems became interested in the subject, but since they were not sympathetic to any spiritual system outside Islam, they confined themselves to the purely chemical side of the new science. For example, under the stimulus of Djabir Ibn Hayyan of Baghdad, a veritable scientific school arose which made important discoveries and established what was eventually to become the basis for Western chemistry. The conquest of southern Spain by the Moors brought alchemy to Europe. It is believed that Italian monks were the first to translate Arab manuscripts into Latin. It is recorded however that in 1144 the English monk, Robert of Chester, translated an Arab work on alchemy.

In Europe, in some cases spurred on by greed, many researchers plunged themselves into ancient alchemical texts, trying to transmute the base metals of tin, lead, copper and iron into silver and gold. Many quacks and charlatans also claimed to have discovered secret formulae for producing an elixir of everlasting life, or gold, thus adding their wild and dishonest imaginings to an already obscure alchemical literature.

In those exciting times, a legend developed about an alchemist named Nicholas Flamel, who many believed had found the secret. According to the legend, Flamel worked for many years without success. One day he discovered an old manuscript containing alchemical symbols which was signed "Abraham the Jew." Flamel invested more years of effort with the help of his wife, a former widow, subsequently known in alchemical history as the "Widow Pernelle," trying to decipher the manuscript. Feeling discouraged, he decided to make the traditional pilgrimage to the Spanish city of Santiago de Compostela, legendary burial place of the Apostle St. James the Martyr, the patron saint of alchemists, taking the manuscript with him. Passing through the city of León he met a mysterious Jew who confided to him the secret of the manuscript. From then on Flamel became very rich, to the extent of granting money to charitable institutions, and contributing to the reconstruction of the Church of St. Jacques-de-Boucheries. Since then no one has ever been able to disprove the story, or offer a satisfactory explanation as to how Flamel came by his fortune.

Alchemy's boom years, in terms of academic interest and

experimentation, were between 1550 and 1650, after which it gradually fell into disrepute because no one managed to demonstrate that the formulae or methods contained in all the different writings on the subject really worked. Despite this, alchemy has continued to fascinate a certain kind of mind, even today, and over the centuries many eminent personalities from all walks of life have been drawn to the Hermetic Art. Paracelsus, Albertus Magnus, Raymond Lull, Roger Bacon, Giordano Bruno, St. Thomas Aquinas, Sir Isaac Newton and Elias Ashmole, one of the fathers of modern Freemasonry, are said to have been practioners.

Paracelsus, famous for his contribution to medicine, is also known as the author of a treatise on alchemy entitled "The Great Mysteries" which was to influence generations of alchemists. Paracelsus was both a medical doctor and metallurgist and tried to apply alchemical methods to medicine. He is considered to be one of the fathers of homoeopathy and was among the first to use the experimental and observational approach to curing disease.

While some of the great minds following in the footsteps of the early Arab researchers have studied alchemy purely from a material point of view, others realized that the purpose of those who developed the process was to provide potential initiates with certain keys which could unlock a secret psycho-spiritual system capable of guiding the persistent practitioner to the summit of spiritual illumination and union with the Divine. These keys are still used today among initiates attracted to this approach. In France, for example, there are a few practising alchemists in the classic mold who are highly respected in esoteric circles. Two of these, personally known to the author, are living proofs that true alchemy, practised by those who know, really works.

Jung, the great Swiss psychoanalyst, has confirmed through practical work on himself and his patients the authentic meaning of alchemy. From his writings, it does not appear that Jung's research took him to the final stage of the alchemical process. He seems to have completed what in alchemy is described as the "Work in the White" after the "Work in the Black." Jung called this the "Individualization of the Personality."

The final step in alchemy is the "Work in the Red," and when this has been carried out successfully one is said to have completed the "Great Work." This is spiritual illumination, the realization of Unity, the acquisition of the Philosopher's Stone. The main obstacle to reaching the summit of the Art is that, as in any other spiritual system, in the final stages of the path the pilgrim has to commit himself totally, sustained only by absolute confidence in the Divine within. It is not recorded how far Jung and his successors approached this final step.

Because of the incredible hotchpotch of influences and deliberate efforts by initiates to conceal the keys to the true techniques, it is virtually impossible to explain in a short summary what alchemy really is. The purpose of the following paragraphs is to give readers who know nothing about alchemy a general introduction to the subject, and to mention a few technical terms which one frequently encounters in esoteric writings.

Like many other approaches dealing with spiritual development, alchemy is really about the nature of transcendental unity and man's urge to integrate himself in it. Aware of the famous axiom of Hermes, or Thoth as he was called in Egypt, the alchemist tries to reproduce in the "philosophical egg" or crucible the same process which gave birth to the world. He does this by attracting Divine grace and then identifying himself with God, after which he proceeds to work in the same way as the Cosmos was created by organizing the primaeval chaos. Although he employs material manipulations to realize his objectives, the goal of the true alchemist is above all spiritual.

The alchemist believes that if he manages to achieve perfection in his art, he will also be transformed in the process, hence the great stress placed in alchemy on the purity of soul and perfection in the application of all the techniques involved in the process.

The alchemists believed that Man had a spirit, an individual soul and a material body. The spirit, which was part of the Universal Spirit, belonged to the Divine world. This spark of the spirit became imprisoned in matter at the time of Man's original fall. In alchemical terminology the body corresponds to salt, the soul to sulphur, and the spirit to mercury, and these three aspects also represent the three universal forces of the Trinity.

The three universal forces operate through seven channels, symbolized by the seven planets. There are seven base metals which correspond to the planets. The Sun corresponds to gold, the Moon to silver, Mercury to mercury, Venus to copper, Mars to iron, Jupiter to tin and Saturn to lead. The world of matter is divided into four elements: Fire, Air, Earth and Water.

In perfecting and redeeming himself, Man also helps the world of Nature to ascend. The Divine has given Man the means whereby he can achieve both spiritual and material perfection. Man is thus able not only to transmute metals; he is also given the means of combating disease and mortality. There is thus an inner alchemy concerned with the perfection of the soul and an outer which concerns the perfecion of matter and the body. Accordingly the quest is oriented in two complemenatry directions. One is the search for the Universal Medicine or Elixir of Long Life. The other is to complete the purification process known as the transmutation of base metals.

The Elixir can only be made after the Philosopher's Stone has been obtained. The Stone, which resembles a ruby, is crushed to a powder, liquified and then drunk. According to alchemical lore, the practitioner will be regenerated by this concoction and will be able to live to the age of 144 without suffering from illness of any kind.

The idea underlying the transmutation of metals is that

metals are living things, and if they are purified to a maximum they will inevitably take the form of gold which is the noblest of all metals. Similarly as the practitioner purifies himself through the frustrations and difficulties encountered in manipulating his alchemical materials, he will reach a certain level of purification in the "Great Work" which will allow him to be restored to Man's original state of purity, i.e. to realize the transmutation to gold within himself. In alchemical jargon he will have discovered the Philosopher's Stone, transcended time and space by dissolving all that is putrescible in his body and being, and coagulating the Divine within him to become one of the elect.

At the end of the process, the two directions of the quest will coalesce. Since both directions are but two sides of the same thing, the outer will become a manifestation of the inner, and the realization of the inner will be facilitated by the perfect execution of the outer. Thus while the principal preoccupation of the true alchemist is not the search for material gold, the process when realized will make the acquisition of gold accessible to him.

Theoretically the alchemist has a choice of three levels of intensity in the speed at which he carries out the quest for the Philosopher's Stone. These are the Wet Process, the Dry Process and the Short Process.

The Wet Process is the most common and is effected by allowing a gradual ripening of the *Materia Prima* or First Matter. The very first alchemical operation is to free the base metal selected as the material for the whole process from its inessential characteristics. When this is done the material becomes the *Materia Prima*. This is then kept in a transparent flask and heated in the *athanor* or alchemical oven, passing through four different phases described successively as Black or Raven, White or Dove, Iridescent or Peacock, Red or Rubification. The Wet Process, if correctly done, will take 40 days.

Information on the Dry Process is only given by word of

mouth. It is known however that it is extremely difficult, and a number of alchemists are said to have died attempting it. The Dry Process is also called the Sacerdotal or Path of the Humble. It is said to take three days. The Short Process takes a few hours or even a few seconds. However, only the very great initiates can accomplish it.

In spiritual terms, the work in the Black or Raven is the descent into the depths of one's being, where one sees both the impure as well as the nobler aspects of oneself. By working on his weaknesses the practitioner masters his lower impulses. In other words by a process of distillation he removes the dross from his basic metals to obtain the *Materia Prima*. This process is also described as capturing and taming the Black Raven. When this operation is successful a quality called the Green Lion followed by another known as the Red Lion will manifest.

In the next stage, the material will develop a white colour which is the philosophical mercury, the mercury of the wise or the Virgin Milk drawn from the May-dew. The final stage is of course the Red stage or Rubification which will bring the desired perfection.

The conditions required for the Great Work are, *inter alia*, solitude, silence, patience, perseverance and discretion. Account also needs to be taken of astrological conditions, and the rules concerning the different stages to be followed in practising the art must be strictly adhered to.

Certain alchemical symbols and ideas form part of the Templar Tradition, which is only natural since many Templars were secret alchemists.

The Castle of Montségur as it is today.

CHAPTER XI
THE CATHARS

THE WORD CATHAR is derived from the Greek word *Catharoi* meaning pure. It is believed to have been first used in the second half of the twelfth century to describe members of a heretical Christian sect which developed in southwestern France and certain other areas in Western Europe during the twelfth and thirteenth centuries. The Cathars were also known as the Albigenses, meaning "Men of Albi." One of the main centers of Catharism was the town of Albi which is today the capital of the County of Tarn, situated about 47 miles northeast of Toulouse. However, there were other heretical sects in the region which were also called Albigenses. In order to understand the meaning of Catharism, a brief mention of the Gnostics, the Manicheans and the Bogomils will be necessary.

The word "Gnosticism" originates from the Greek *gnostikos* which means one who has *gnosis* or knowledge. Gnosticism is an ancient religious movement which predates Christianity but which subsequently interacted with it during the first three centuries of the Christian era.

The basic doctrine of gnosticism is dualism, though the degree and nuances of the doctrine have varied throughout its history. Dualism is the belief that there are two creative forces: God the Absolute who created the spiritual world, and a lower being who created the evil material world. According to this doctrine, there is an aspect of man, of which he is not normally conscious, which is part of the Godhead itself. Because of the Fall this became captive in matter. Through an initiatory experience bringing revelation from above, Man can become aware of his divinity and destiny and thereby regain his original world of the spirit. This realization cannot be achieved through studying sacred books or doctrine; it can only come through inner revelation.

One of the effects of Christian influence was to encourage a certain flexibility among different Gnostic groups as to the relationship between God and the created world. Probably the main effect of Gnosticism on Christianity was to oblige the latter to develop a doctrine to counter the concept of dualism and to assert the importance of the work of Jesus Christ.

The term Gnosis is frequently encountered in hermetic and esoteric teachings. Modern Gnosticism is no longer dualistic, and the word Gnosis is used nowadays generally to mean the realization of one's divinity through inner revelation rather than through mastery of a given doctrine.

The original Gnostics accepted the idea of the Christ within but rejected the atonement. To them the Christ was a great prophet who had realized the Gnosis. One of the better known sources of Gnostic doctrine is the *Pistis Sophia,* and as it was written in the third century, it shows considerable Christian influence. This work takes the form of a dialogue betwen Jesus and his disciples along with Mary Magdalene on the Mount of Olives, 11 years after the crucifixion. *Pistis Sophia* is the World Soul which has fallen with Man and can be redeemed by Man if he redeems himself.

The Manichean sect was founded by Manes, a Persian mystic who lived between 215 and 276 AD. Manes was initiated into the Mysteries of Mithras, and although he is reputed to have studied those mystical teachings of esoteric Judaism which were to become the Cabala, his own teachings were very much influenced by Gnosticism, of which he adopted a very radical form. He taught that the material world and the spiritual world were completely separate. The spiritual world, which was good, was created by God, and the material world, which was evil, was created by Satan. Man contained the goodness of the spiritual world within him, and his main purpose in life was to free his spirit from the evil world of matter so that it could return to God.

Manes taught that Jesus as a personality was neither the unique son of God nor the provider of salvation. Jesus, according to Manes, came to show the way, demonstrating that the Christ within him and within all human beings was the only hope of salvation.

Manes ran into opposition from the Zoroastrians and was eventually tortured and crucified. After the death of Manes, the inner circle of his followers organized and promoted the sect so effectively that it soon spread through Turkestan, parts of the Middle East and as far as India and China.

Manicheism was adopted betwen the tenth and fifteenth centuries by a number of people living in the Balkan region known today as Bulgaria. The Bulgarian version of Manicheism was named after its founder, Bogomil. During the eleventh and twelfth centuries, the movement spread throughout many European and Asian provinces of the Byzantine Empire. The strong reactions against heresy at the time brought persecution, and in 1100 the leaders of Bogomilism were imprisoned and their leader Basil burned to death. About 1150 the influence of the Bogomils began to be felt in parts of France and Italy. In Bulgaria itself they remained a powerful influence until about the fourteenth century, when the Ottoman conquest brought the movement to an end.

The Albigensian movement and Catharism were at first not just a branch of Bogomil Manicheism; there were already doctrinal trends in that direction in southern France. The Bogomil movement strengthened and gave more systematic and organized form to these heretical tendencies, but around 1150 the situation changed considerably and the doctrines of the Bogomils became closely associated with Catharism. Nicetas, a Bogomil bishop, visited the south of France in 1167.

Ironically, Bernard of Clairvaux was called into the breach to persuade the Cathars to return to the Catholic fold. Even he was not successful and they proceeded to organize themselves into a church. Shortly afterwards a large number of bishops were appointed in Albi and others later in Toulouse, Carcassonne and Val d'Aran. A number of bishoprics were also established in Italy.

In 1209 Pope Innocent III obliged the Cistercians to preach a crusade against the Cathars. A civil war took place in which the Provencal civilization of southern France, including Toulouse, was destroyed. The Cathars and other Albigenses survived only to be crushed later by the Inquisition in 1239. In 1244 the fortress of Montségur, the main Cathar stronghold, was captured and destroyed, and large numbers of Cathars burnt alive. The surviving Cathars had to go underground and many fled to Italy, where persecution was less intense.

The Dominican and Franciscan Orders were founded in the thirteenth century to counteract the influence of the Cathars. Their respective techniques were different but equally effective. The Dominicans evolved techniques which developed into the Inquisition, while the Franciscans preached and won over the masses with the message that the world was God's and therefore good. An interesting point in passing: St. Augustine was once a member of the Manichean sect, but when he embraced Roman Catholicism he became one of the sect's most ardent enemies.

In the way they lived the Cathars were very similar to the Essenes, and even their detractors had to admit that they were very pure people. At one stage there developed a divergence of doctrine within the Bogomil churches, between those who took a more moderate view on dualism and those who wished to follow a more radical line. The Cathars supported the radical form of dualism.

In the practice of their beliefs, the Cathars were extremely ascetic. Meat and sexual intercourse were forbidden. In order to accommodate those believers who were not able to follow the very strict discipline of Catharism, a division was introduced whereby those who followed the discipline completely were known as *Parfaits,* or Perfect Ones. The latter were set apart from the others by an initiation ceremony which involved the breaking of bread. The Cathars incidentally did not believe in transubstantiation. As far as the Holy Scriptures were concerned, the Cathars did not completely accept the Old Testament and had their own interpretations of some parts of the New Testament. The Cathars also believed, like the Manicheans, that one's spiritual being remained in heaven and could be united with one's soul (which was attached to the physical body) only through a revealed spiritual knowledge—Gnosis. If this Gnosis were not realized, one's spiritual being would be obliged to attach itself to another physical body when the existing body died.

The legacy of the Cathars was not merely the memory of their purity and their courage. They and other heretical sects laid the foundation for what became Protestantism. There was also an esoteric side to the Cathars linked to the legend of the Holy Grail. According to the Tradition certain of the *Parfaits* decided to perpetuate their secret teachings by disguising themselves as troubadours, peddlars, merchants and craftsmen and to discreetly pass on their teachings in the course of their wanderings. It is also claimed that they infiltrated the guilds, the remnants of Templarism and Compagnonage, and later the Freemasons.

Wagner's *Tannhauser* and *Parsifal* were based on the Grail stories accredited to Wolfram von Eschenbach, who almost certainly came into contact with Cathars whilst practising his calling. There is the legend referred to earlier which states that when Montségur was about to be taken by the armies of Innocent III, the Cathars secretly sent away their sacred relics to be hidden in a safe place. According to this legend one of these relics was a chalice which, if it was not the original Grail, was reputed to have had the qualities of the Grail.

Various researchers have tried to trace links between the Knights Templar and the Cathars but the evidence is not clear. It appears that some Templars were obliged to take part in attacks against the Cathars. It is also claimed that some

Templars managed to avoid taking part and even provided hiding places for Cathars who wished to escape persecution. There is no clear evidence of direct contacts for the sharing of their respective experiences. It is reasonable to assume, however, that if the Cathars had any teaching which could have added to the collection of knowledge the Templars sought to preserve, it is likely that the Templars would have availed themselves of it.

CHAPTER XII
THE COMPAGNONS

COMPAGNONAGE was the name given in France to certain guilds with mystical associations, formed between workmen in the building trade to promote their mutual interests. The basis of each guild was called the *Devoir* or duty. The Devoir was the collection of rules, work practices, traditions and rites of the craft. The essence of Compagnonage was to promote a workmen's elite which would bring a deeper dimension to manual work through the attitude that there was much more to the practice of a craft than earning a living.

Although virtually no mention of Compagnonage has been found in public documents of the early Middle Ages, it can be traced back to at least the twelfth century. At that time it came to public notice in the form of associations founded to protect workmen during their travels, and to provide friendly contact for members arriving in strange towns. One of the earliest official references to them is in 1420, in an ordinance during the reign of Charles VI.

There were three main associations deriving from three traditions:

The Children of Solomon
The Children of Master Jacques
The Children of Father Soubise

The Children of Solomon claimed that Solomon gave them their Devoir as a reward for their work during the building of the Temple, and that he had united them in a brotherhood. The Children of Master Jacques traced their origins to one of the Master Builders who was a colleague of Hiram Abiff, the great builder sent to King Solomon by Hiram, King of Tyre, to supervise the building of the temple. Father Soubise, the legend goes, was a colleague of Master Jacques, and after the temple was completed they travelled together to Gaul, swearing that they would never part. Their association did not last because of rivalry, and Master Jacques was murdered by certain disciples of Father Soubise who himself denied any involvement. Another legend claims that Master Jacques was in reality Jacques de Molay, the last Grand Master of the Knights Templar.

Within each of the three associations there was a system of initiations and degrees with secret signs, passwords and decorations. At least during the time of the Templars, there was also a system of secret instruction. The art of building and the esoteric knowledge associated with it were passed on only by word of mouth. The first stage of membership was that of Apprentice, which lasted about five years before arriving at the stage of *Mâitrise* or Mastership. As soon as a craftsman finished his apprenticeship he joined one of the three associations and commenced an obligatory journey through France, known in the tradition as the *Tour de France.*

The Compagnon survived during the Tour by working as he went. In each town there was a "House" of the association presided over by a woman called the "Mother." Meetings were held in the House, officers were elected and food and lodging offered there to travelling members.

There were very strict rules concerning communal life, such as respect for the elders of the craft, for the Mother of the House, and for all Compagnons regardless of religion, race or political opinions. At table in the communal House, all conversation which could lead to discord was forbidden. Anyone who did not respect this rule was subject to a fine which was adjusted according to the importance of the fault. Before sitting at table the Compagnons had to satisfy the Mother that they were suitably dressed. They also had to ask permission to leave the table and were liable to fines if they were late for supper.

The Compagnons had many quaint customs, practices and dress. They also developed a vocabulary of their own. The word *coterie* for example was a generic term used to designate a given *devoir*, the different functions performed or the grade reached within a trade. A "Dog" was a compagnon who had completed his *Tour de France*, a "Fox" was an aspirant, and a "Monkey" was a Master Craftsman.

Chapter VI has already suggested how the mutual influences of the Templars and the Compagnons might have acted and reacted on each other. For example, the Templars certainly deepened the spiritual dimension of the artisans' contact with forms and materials. The Compagnon provided the constructions to be ensouled by the laws and spiritual principles taught and practiced by the Templars.

Compagnonage has had to adapt itself to a variety of historical circumstances. The movement was persecuted from the fall of the Templars all the way down to the nineteenth century. Ironically, the Renaissance did not work in its favor since one of its legacies was the introduction of the speculative element in artistic creation, whereby the artist imposed his own inspiration and assigned a secondary role to the purely manual aspect of the work. The public became interested only in the artist who conceived a building or a sculpture and not in the artisans who carried out the basic physical work.

The sixteenth century Reformation, the democratic ideals of the French Revolution of 1789 and the popular movements of the 1800's were also not conducive to the Compagnon's way of life. In the industrial era, although there has been no persecution of Compagnonage, the by-products of socialism and trade unionism have not helped it either. Although Compagnonage was not attached to any particular religion, it was religious in the sense that it did not consider man a purely economic being, but a composite unit linked to a universe with which he sought harmony through the search for form. This approach was not very popular in the rising materialism of the late nineteenth century. All these external pressures were bound to react unfavorably on the internal unity of the Compagnon movement. From the sixteenth century onwards the movement began to break up and all kinds of dissension arose.

During the Reformation a split developed. There were the *Gavots* who followed the reformers, and the *Devorants* who stayed faithful to the Catholic Church. Problems on the building site of Orleans Cathedral brought matters to a head and created what was subsequently called the Schism of Orleans. The revocation of the Edict of Nantes in 1685 accelerated the division and decline of the movement and many Compagnons who were Protestants emigrated to Germany, Switzerland and other countries. Even the traditional *Tour de France* was banned by Louis XIV.

In 1793 some of those Compagnons who belonged to the Devoir of Father Soubise decided to drop all religious elements from the association, an action which resulted in the formation of a new Devoir called the Devoir of Liberty. The nineteenth century was a particularly agitated time within what remained of Compagnonage. After several failures the Compagnon Union was set up in 1889, bringing together the different groupings. This did not last and the Union disappeared at the end of the nineteenth century.

In France today, Compagnonage operates principally within the framework of the Workers Association of the Compagnons of Duty, the Compagnon Federation of Building Trades and an earlier version of the Compagnon Union which had been founded in 1875, and was later temporarily incorporated into the Union referred to above. In recent years there have been glimmerings of interest in Europe, especially in West Germany, Belgium, Switzerland and the Scandinavian countries, among the younger generation who are attracted to the idea of becoming master craftsmen of a trade. Regrettably, there may no longer be enough true masters of the crafts capable of transmitting the spiritual tradition which inspired the original Compagnons.

CHAPTER XIII

THE ROSICRUCIANS AND THE ROSE-CROIX

The Rosicrucians

IT IS NOT possible to explain Rosicrucianism in a simple, straightforward manner. As is the case with so many of the subjects dealt with in this book accounts of its characteristics and history are a mixture of facts, fables, legends and sometimes deliberate invention. It is even uncertain when the word "Rosicrucianism" was first used. As a belief system, it came to the notice of the general public in the seventeenth century when an anonymous work now known as the *Fama*, mentioning a mysterious personage called Christian Rosenkreutz, was published. The German word *Rosenkreutz* means "rosy cross." Before running through what is generally known about Rosicrucianism, it might be useful to look at the symbolism of the Rose and the Cross to see why they were chosen as the name of this legendary personality.

The Rose and the Cross are very profound symbols in the sense that if we meditate or even think about them, they affect us deeply. Like the symbol of the Grail, regular meditation on the Rose and the Cross can have very strong effects on our inner lives.

Let us begin with the Cross. No single culture or religion can claim to be the originator of the Cross as a symbol. It is found in all religions and cultures from time immemorial, and belongs to the common heritage of all mankind. In Jungian terms the Cross is one of the basic symbols through which that "data bank," the collective unconscious, containing the accumulated knowledge of the evolutionary experience of the human race, tries to convey to us certain aspects of transcendental reality.

In ancient civilizations, the Cross was a schematic representation of the insertion of the microcosm within the macrocosm. That is to say, the Cross was considered by the ancients as an affirmation of the existence of man as a miniature of the cosmos possessing the same structure and animated by the same cyclical impulse of creative force.

Down through the ages the Cross has evolved in many forms. The oldest is the equal-armed cross known as the *Crux Quadrata;* then there is the Latin Cross or *Crux Inmisa;* the Egyptian Cross or *Crux Ansata;* the Celtic Cross *et cetera.*

Whenever most people think of the Cross they tend to think of the crucifixion. In fact the Cross existed long before the crucifixion. In early times, for example, the equal—armed cross represented the four cardinal points and the four alchemical elements of Earth, Water, Fire and Air. The Cross also symbolizes the union of the active masculine principle which is vertical, and the passive feminine principle which is horizontal. If the human body is envisaged standing with feet together and arms outstretched horizontally, the image would correspond exactly to the design of the Latin Cross, corroborating the symbolism of the insertion of man into the cosmos represented by the four cardinal points.

In the astrological tradition, the twelve signs of the Zodiac are arranged in such a way that three signs are placed on each of the four cardinal points, each point representing one of the four elements. This arrangement was known in antiquity as the "Rose of the Winds," with the probable connotation that it was the Cross of the Four Elements which when brought into equilibrium will permit the Wind of the Spirit or the Rose to blossom forth. One could also stretch the symbolism further by visualizing the Cross as spinning on its axis, pushed by the creative, cyclical and evolutionary Wind of the Spirit to delineate time and space, the necessary conditions for material manifestation.

The spread of the Rose as a flower in the West was probably due to the arrival of the Arabs in the Iberian Peninsula. It subsequently became part of the culture of many nations and is prominently encountered in literature, music, painting, embroidery, heraldry, legends and religion. This was due to an almost universal appreciation of its qualities of elegance and beauty, which have made it the ideal symbol of nobility, love and perfection.

The Red Rose came to symbolize the passion of love or the passion of suffering. The average rose, in the Middle Ages, was probably a spindly shrub. Suffering was symbolized by this shrub's struggle to transform gross material nourishment from the earth to produce its beautiful flower, a flower so delicate that it had to be surrounded by thorns. The red color of the Rose also symbolizes the red fire of the spirit which pushes man to perfect himself in the crucible of material life—the Cross of the Four Elements. The Rose was used in the Middle Ages as a secret sign by many members of spiritual and intellectual movements that dared to question the beliefs of the established church. For these free thinkers, it represented the fragile flame of awareness with the aid of which the hidden truths of Universal Harmony might be rediscovered. Even Martin Luther, one of the fathers of the Reformation, adopted the cross with a rose in the center as his personal emblem.

According to 'the French writer Gérard de Sède in his books *La Rose-Croix* and *Le Secret des Cathares*, the first time an emblem combining the Rose and the Cross was publicly displayed was in eleventh century Spain in the independent kingdom of Aragon.

There is a legend surrounding this event according to which an Aragonese Knight named Iñigo Arista, in the midst of a fierce battle against the Moors, suddenly saw a cross of light in the sky with a rose on each of its arms. Taking this to be a sign from God that his side would triumph, Arista plunged with great determination into the fray, from which the Aragonese emerged victorious. A monastery to commemorate this event was erected near the site and dedicated to St. John. This is the monastery of San Juan de la Peña, which today can be found near the town of Jaca in the Province of Huesca. Some time later an Order of Chivalry with the emblem of the Roses and the Cross was founded in the monastery.

Gérard de Sède writes that there is a historical record which relates that in 1623, the agents of the French King Louis XIII mentioned in a report that members of a secret Rosicrucian fraternity participated in a solemn ceremony at each Feast of St. John in San Juan de la Peña. In the monastery today one can see a painting depicting the legend of Iñigo Arista, as well as the tombs of twenty-four Knights of St. John, each decorated with the four Roses and the Cross.

The unusual character of this historic site and the gentle beauty of the countryside in the surrounding provinces of Huesca and Navarre makes a trip to the region a "must" for spiritually minded travellers planning a visit to Spain. San Juan de la Peña is really a huge cave converted into a monastery. It is impressive not only because of the grandeur of its setting and its unusual construction, but because the atmosphere of what was undoubtedly a place of high spirituality still lingers in spite of a recent extensive program of restoration. Who knows what a respectful pilgrim to the monastery may have experienced there?

Returning to the history of the Rose and the Cross, Gerard de Sède also mentions that the banner of Raymond VI, Count of Toulouse, who tried to defend the Cathars against the armies of Innocent III, was in the form of a cross, described in heraldry as *de gueules à la croix et pommettée d'or.* In heraldry *gueule* means red and was derived from the Arabic word *gul* meaning rose. De Sède sees a link in the fact that at the time, Aragon was the most loyal ally of Toulouse in its fight against the papal army led by Simon de Montfort.

Against this rich tapestry of history, legend and symbolism, it can be seen why the Cross with the red Rose in the center, representing man's noblest aspirations, was adopted as the emblem of the Rosicrucian movement. Its basic tenets, which stem from the distant past, are shared by other spiritual groups but its true origins lie hidden in the records of secret fraternities, with the result that writers have given different versions of its history and of the often enigmatic personalities who are known to have been its emissaries.

There are many Rosicrucian orders, lodges and societies. Some are secret, others operate quite publicly. All claim to possess secret teachings handed down from a secret brotherhood. These teachings appear to be a combination of various currents of the Tradition such as Gnosticism, Alchemy or Hermeticism and Cabalism. At their best these orders declare themselves to be seekers after truth whose aim is to help humanity free itself from the thrall of material darkness.

Certain writers have used the word Rosicrucianism to describe the movements and ideas which followed the publication in Cassel, Germany, between 1614 and 1616, of the three works generally referred to as "The Rosicrucian Manifestos." The first was the famous *Fama Fraternitatis,* followed by the *Confessio* and the *Chymical Marriage of Christian Rosenkreutz.* Their full titles were:

The Fama Fraternitatis or *Laudable Fraternity of the Rosy Cross*

The Confessio Fraternitatis or *Confession of the Laudable Fraternity of the Most Honourable Order of the Rosy Cross*

The Chymical Marriage of Christian Rosenkreutz in the year 1549.

The first two works were written in the form of declarations, while the third was an alchemical text. The *Fama* describes the founding of the Fraternity of the Rosy Cross by Christian Rosenkreutz, after his journeys to Damascus, Damcar in Arabia, Egypt and Fez in Morocco. In these cities he met those who were in possession of secret teachings in philosophy, magic and Cabalism. After synthesizing the best of the teachings he received, Rosenkreutz went to Spain to meet other learned men in the hope of sharing his knowledge with them but he was not taken seriously. Returning to Germany, he chose three other men with whom he founded an order after instructing them in the knowledge he had obtained in the Middle East.

The number was eventually increased to eight, upon which five were sent separately into different countries. Before leaving, each member of the fraternity agreed that he would not follow any profession other than that of healing the sick, and this should be done free of charge; that he would follow the customs of the country where he was sent, and would not draw attention to himself by adopting any particular style of dress; that every year on a certain day he would meet with the others in the house where it all began and which they called the House of the Holy Spirit, or submit his reason in writing; that he would prepare someone to succeed him on his death; that their seal should be the word C.R.; and finally, that the Fraternity should remain secret for one hundred years.

It was also agreed that on the death of Christian Rosenkreutz his body should be placed in a secret vault where it should remain hidden for one hundred and twenty years. The document goes on to state that at the end of this period, a member of the Order found the secret vault, containing the perfectly preserved body of the founder and a number of precious documents and symbols. The vault was then closed, and the Order dispersed.

According to the *Confessio*, Christian Rosenkreutz was born in 1378 and lived 106 years. Most writers are of the opinion that the story of the life and death of Christian Rosenkreutz was a symbolic explanation of the Order and that Christian Rosenkreutz was the pseudonym for several of its members. Some believe that while the first two works were a collective effort, the *Chymical Marriage of Christian Rosenkreutz* was written by Johann-Valentin Andreae, who lived from 1586 to 1654. In his old age Andreae denied authorship and claimed that he had never been a member of a Rosicrucian fraternity, but later historians have pointed to the fact that his family crest contained a red cross with four roses, and also that the social ideas which he advocated and the way he lived conformed very much to the Rosicrucian ideal. It is also known that in genuine Rosicrucian orders, members are required by rule not to reveal their identity.

After the publication of the Manifestos, many Rosicrucian orders and belief-systems influenced by their approach to life developed in Europe. This movement followed two streams. There was a current of ideas developed by a number of scientists, intellectuals and reformers in the social, political and philosophical fields which was characterized by a Utopian vision of the world. The other aspect was the Hermetic and Cabalistic type of Rosicrucianism, which was concerned essentially with occultism and mysticism.

Two well-known members of the Utopian school were René Descartes (1596-1650) and Robert Boyle (1626-1691). Rosicrucians who chose the Hermetic path included Thomas Vaughan, born 1622, and Thomas Heydon (1629-1667). There were of course individuals who were active in both aspects of Rosicrucianism such as Francis Bacon (1561-1626), Thomas Campanella (1568-1639), Robert Fludd (1574-1637), Jan Comenius (1592-1670), and Elias Ashmole (1617-1692).

There is a belief that Francis Bacon was the real author of the more profound of Shakespeare's works. There are writers who claim that some of the latter's writings such as *Love's Labours Lost* showed some familiarity with Rosicrucian ideas, and that the only man in England who could have written them was Bacon. The fact that *Love's Labours Lost* was first produced in 1595 before the publication of the *Fama* was shrugged off by the pro-Bacon school, who have pointed out that this meant nothing since the original Rosicrucian Order must have existed before the *Fama* was published. There is another view that Bacon and Shakespeare were simply members of the same Rosicrucian Order.

In the case of Descartes, it is known that he was very much

influenced by Rosicrucian ideas and had tried very hard to contact the Order. Descartes' difficulty stemmed from the fact that the French, in general, had reacted negatively to the great interest which was shown throughout Europe in the publication of the *Fama*. One day in 1623 notices were put up in Paris purporting to be the work of a secret Rosicrucian brotherhood. The text of the notices was as follows:

"We, the deputies of the Head College of the Rosy Cross, now sojourning visible and invisible, in this city, by grace of the Most High towards Whom the hearts of sages turn, do teach without the help of books, or signs, how to speak the language of every country wherein we elect to stay, in order that we may rescue our fellow men from the error of death."

The notice quoted above brought considerable opposition to Rosicrucian ideas. There are differences of view among specialists of Rosicrucian history as to whether the Paris notices were hoaxes or really the work of Rosicrucian adepts, and the relationship between Descartes and the movement has never been clearly established.

It was in France that Rosicrucianism was to have a revival which climaxed between the early nineteenth and the first years of the twentieth century. Some of the well-known names associated with this revival are Martinez de Pasqually (1727-1774), Cagliostro (1743-1795), Louis-Claude de Saint Martin (1743-1803), Josephin Péladan (1859-1918), Gérard Encausse, also known as Papus (1865-1918), and Stanislaus de Guaita (1861-1897).

Péladan's brand of Rosicrucianism became very popular among artistic circles at France in the beginning of this century. In 1892 he sponsored a series of artistic exhibitions called the *Salons de la Rose-Croix.* Some of the well- known artists who had connections with the movement were the painters Gustave Moreau and Georges Rouault and the composer Erik Satie. A number of present-day groups in America claim to derive their authority from various branches of the French Rosicrucian movement.

Harvey Spencer Lewis (1883-1934), founder of the modern Rosicrucian movement in America (AMORC), advanced a history of the Rosicrucians, in which he claimed that the movement was established in ancient Egypt by the Pharaoh Tutmosis III and perpetuated by the great Amenhotep IV, better known as Akhenaton.

According to Spencer Lewis, seventeenth-century Rosicrucianism was merely the external manifestation of an Order that had never lost its continuity, despite its tradition of operating in cycles of 108 years of activity and 108 years of silence in any given country. It is claimed by AMORC that in accordance with this tradition, Spencer Lewis was delegated to begin a new cycle of activity in the United States in 1915.

The Rose-Croix

In the Temple tradition a distinction is made between a "Rose-Croix" and a "Rosicrucian." The word Rose-Croix is used to differentiate between a person who has reached a level which foreshadows the next important stage of the evolution of humanity, and someone who is merely a member of a Rosicrucian order or movement. A Rose-Croix has been described as someone whose spiritual attainment has enabled him or her to obtain practical knowledge of the secret significance of the Rose and the Cross.

According to the Temple tradition such rare individuals do not obtain their authority from any type of organization, though they have used orders or movements to transmit their ideas. Some of these individuals have fulfilled their mission posing as ordinary personalities, and the knowledge of their true identities and the extent of their contribution to the evolution of humanity has died with them. Of this handful of beings the only known figures who were confirmed by the Tradition were Cagliostro and the mysterious Comte de Saint Germain.

Despite the strange personality he presented to the world,

it is now accepted in esoteric circles that Cagliostro was not the rascal and mountebank which popular history made him out to be, but was one of the great men of the eighteenth century. He is now considered to have been secretly behind many ideas which influenced the spiritual, social, and political thought of his time. It is said that he affected his particular personality because it enabled him to become the confidant of people in high places, and thereby indirectly to influence events.

The Comte de St. Germain is reported to have astounded his eighteenth century contemporaries with his longevity, knowledge and strange powers. Like Cagliostro he managed to move in circles where he was able to influence kings and rulers from behind the scenes.

Raymond Bernard, the French Rosicrucian, mentions in his book *Rencontres avec l'insolite* a mysterious Rose-Croix called Maha whom he apparently encountered from time to time in different European countries. Some contemporary works dealing with Rosicrucianism refer to the existence of a secret fraternity—The Elder Brothers of the Rose-Croix—which is said to faithfully follow the tradition as outlined in the *Fama*.

The esoteric Tradition considers the Rosicrucian movement as one of the manifestations of the eternal Temple. A genuine order of the Temple today should be able to transmit, along with other teachings of the primordial wisdom, the essential message of the true Rose-Croix. This does not mean of course that one can expect to find Rose-Croix adepts behind every worthy esoteric order. Rather the ideals and inspiration of the Rose-Croix should be present in a genuine order, in ways which will permit members to progressively approach this high state of spiritual realization.

In conclusion, despite its flowery eighteenth century style, not many better descriptions of the state of being of a Rose-Croix can be found than the following statement attributed to Cagliostro:

"I hail from no particular epoch or place; beyond time and

space my spiritual being lives its eternal existence and, if I turn my mind within, remounting the stream of the ages, and extend my consciousness towards a state of being far beyond that which you can perceive, I become whoever I desire. Consciously participating in the Absolute Being, I adapt my actions according to where I find myself. My name is that of my function and I choose them both because I am free: my country is where momentarily I halt my steps. You may pride yourselves on the past glories of your ancestors, who are strangers to you; or you may give yourself importance with illusory thoughts of future glory, which alas, may never be yours; I, I am he who Is. I was born not of the flesh but of the spirit. My name which is of me and from me, the one which I have chosen in order to appear amongst you, is that which I claim. That which I was given at birth, that which I was called in my youth, like those from other times and places I have left behind, discarding them as I would discard unfashionable clothes, now become useless.

"Here I stand—a Noble Traveller; I speak and your soul trembles, recognizing words from long ago; a voice within you, long silenced, responds to my call; I act, and peace returns to your hearts, health to your bodies, hope and courage to your souls. All men are my brothers, all lands I hold dear; I journey through them so that everywhere I pass the Spirit may descend and find its way to you. Of kings, whose power I respect, I ask but the hospitality of their lands, and where this is granted me I pass, doing as much good as I can, but merely pass. Am I not a Noble Traveller?

"Like the South wind, like the dazzling light of the midday sun which characterizes the full awareness of things and active communion with God, I am heading North to the mist and the cold, leaving in my wake parts of myself, exhausting and diminishing my energies at each resting place, but leaving you a little light, a little warmth, a little strength, until finally it is finished, and I will have reached the end of my journey, the hour when the Rose will bloom on the Cross. I am Cagliostro . . ."

CHAPTER XIV
THE FREEMASONS

THE HISTORY of Freemasonry is even more complex and misunderstood than some of the subjects dealt with hitherto. The writer will nevertheless try to explain a few of its basic elements which relate directly to the Templar tradition.

It is believed that the word "Mason" was originally derived from an old French word *maçonner*. The word was apparently used to designate a craftsman who worked in stone. It is certain that the word mason was used as early as the thirteenth century.

There are different versions of how the word "Freemason" evolved. One of these versions states that it was a term applied to those masons who were free to exercise their trade in a particular municipality; another is that it referred to those specially qualified builders who worked in "free stone" or ornamental stones, and who possessed some architectural knowledge, as opposed to masons who did not prepare the stone but performed the purely physical task of, for example, lifting and putting the stone in place. There is reported to be a document dated 1375 relating to a meeting of municipal guilds in London which uses the word freemason.

These craftsmen or freemasons gradually formed mutual help associations which were taken over by more intellectually-minded people in the eighteenth century. This brought to Masonry what is now called the speculative element as opposed to actual physical practice of the craft.

Specialists in Masonic history seem to agree that the first case in which a "non-operative" was admitted was that of John Boswell of Auchinleck in May 1640 in Edinburgh, Scotland. The Rosicrucian Elias Ashmole, one of the great scholars of his time, was admitted as a non-operative Mason in 1641. It is still not clear why intellectuals were attracted by a working man's association, nor how they managed to introduce a spiritual rather than an artisanal orientation to the development of the movement.

One explanation as to why Freemasonry developed a speculative character could be that men belonging to secret esoteric orders with Templar or Rosicrucian antecedents might have considered these associations to be ideal channels for popularizing ideas for the spiritual and moral betterment of mankind.

Symbols are considered by Masons to be very effective ways of conveying the essential ideas of what Masonry stands for. Symbols appeal directly to the deeper level of our beings, and as Masons everywhere use the same symbols they consider them to be universal and unifying devices which, by continuously reminding members of basic truths, obviate the need for long speeches on Masonic ideals and morality.

The Temple of Solomon is one of the basic symbols of Freemasonry. It is conceived as representing the three principles of man and the universe, i.e. Spirit, Soul and Body. Solomon's Temple contained three sections—a Holy of Holies which only the High Priest could enter on special days; a sanctuary enclosing the Holy of Holies; and a third section where the ordinary worshippers could congregate. The two pillars at the entrance to the Temple are called *Jachin* and *Boaz* respectively. Jachin is the right-hand pillar usually of a light colour, and Boaz the left-hand pillar of dark colour. The right-hand pillar represents the positive polarity of manifestation and the left-hand pillar the negative polarity, or, respectively, the active masculine principle and the passive feminine principle.

The arch or "Royal Arch" joining the two pillars at the top represents the heavens. The floor of the Temple is traditionally decorated in black and white squares representing the earth and symbolizing again the two principles of polarity. Two other important Masonic symbols are the Square and the Compass. Three lights are supposed to be present in a Masonic Temple.

One is the Light Above or belief in the moral order of the world; this is represented in Masonic temples by the Bible. the Square represents the Light Within us or moral conduct, and the Compass represents the Light Around us or the idea of fraternity or service to mankind. Freemasonry is full of other symbols, many of which it has in common with the Rosicrucian tradition. Another evidence of Rosicrucian influence in Masonry is the adoption by French Masonry of a grade known as the Rose-Croix.

Freemasonry as a movement is considered to have made its official appearance in 1717 when four existing lodges combined to form a Grand Lodge. Many of the stories concerning Masonic beginnings are considered to be legendary and may have been invented originally to give an ancient air of venerable respectability to the movement. Among the prominent figures of Masonic legends are Hiram Abiff, King Solomon's Master Builder, and Jabal, Jubal and Tubal-Cain, the sons of Lamech, also the father of Noah. Jabal was supposed to have been the inventor of geometry and the builder of the first stone house, Jubal the discoverer of music, and Tubal-Cain the first worker in metals.

Freemasonry was condemned by Pope Clément XIII, who promulgated the first Anti-Masonic Bull in 1738. Any Catholic who joined a Masonic organization was liable to excommunication. The Pope considered Freemasonry a pagan institution, an idea which was shared by some Protestants.

The history and complexity of Freemasonry cannot be adequately dealt with in the space available here. As a movement it still exists and in the last few centuries many of the most powerful and famous people have been Freemasons.

Some people however continue to view it with suspicion, regarding it as something not quite acceptable; others look upon it as a kind of harmless association of quaint people who enjoy old rituals and perform some benevolent work. And there are yet others who believe that while the vast majority of Masons are only concerned with the external forms of Freemasonry, a small number of masonic groups exist that understand and apply the essence of the Tradition inherited directly or indirectly from the strands of esoteric knowledge mentioned in this book.

CHAPTER XV
THE ORDER OF THE GOLDEN DAWN

IN 1865 AN ENGLISHMAN named Robert Wentforth Little founded an esoteric society—The Rosicrucian Society—in Anglia. Membership was deliberately limited and only Freemasons who had reached the grade of Master Mason were allowed to join. The nineteenth century novelist and politician, Edward Bulwer Lytton, author of the successful historical novel *The Last Days of Pompeii*, and the Rosicrucian romance *Zanoni*, was one of the senior officers of the Society.

After Wentworth Little's death in 1878, three men took over the running of the Society. They were a retired medical doctor, William Woodman (1828-1891), a coroner, Dr. Wynn Westcott (1848-1925), and Samuel MacGregor Mathers (1854-1918).

In 1887, so the story goes, the Reverend A.F.A. Woodward, an elderly parson and author on Freemasonry, gave a coded manuscript which he found in a London public library to Wynn Westcott. The origins of this document have never been established, and Woodward himself died in December of that year. Westcott deciphered the document and found that it contained the outlines of a series of rituals for a group which called itself the Golden Dawn. What transpired immediately after this event has been the subject of heated debate ever since.

What is certain is that Westcott asked Mathers and Woodman to join with him in setting up a new esoteric order, which would derive its inspiration from the rituals found in the document. They agreed, and the Hermetic Order of the Golden Dawn was established in 1887/88. The official history of the Order claims that the address of a German initiate in

Berlin called Anna Sprangel was found in the deciphered document. When contacted, she gave Westcott authority to set up an English branch of the long-established secret esoteric order to which she belonged.

Some historians in this field claim that in order to give an authentic background to his new order, Westcott invented the story of Anna Sprangel. Whatever the truth of the matter, a series of systematic study instructions including lessons on the Cabala and Hermetic Symbolism were drawn up, a system of initiations and grades established, and a hierarchy of officers appointed. Mathers undertook the development of what were to become the Golden Dawn rituals. Shortly after an inner Order was added to which only the most advanced members could belong.

The order was very well administered by Westcott with Mathers supplying the inspiration. Membership increased rapidly and by the end of 1891 when one of the triumvirate—Woodman—died, there were some 81 members in the London Lodge alone. Some of the well-known people who joined the Golden Dawn were the writers Arthur Machen, Bram Stoker and W.B. Yeats; Gerald Kelly, the president of the Royal Society; the Masonic expert Arthur Edward Waite; and one of the most famous actresses of the time, Florence Farr.

In 1892 Mathers produced a new ritual for the inner order based on the myth of Christian Rosenkreutz as related in the *Fama*. He also reformed the Order with himself as head, and introduced more practical work, which made membership of the inner order even more demanding. Even his detractors admit that the training followed in the inner Order was extremely thorough and that those who managed to stay the course ended up with a very good grounding in almost every aspect of the Western Esoteric Tradition.

The Order's best years were 1891-1896. After this the personalities of Mathers and Westcott clashed, and the Order declined rapidly with members splitting off to form rival orders.

The Golden Dawn did not have a good press during the years of its internal convulsions, nor in the years immediately following the first World War. The public antics of Aleister Crowley, a former member who subsequently set up his own order, did not help the image of the Golden Dawn, despite the fact that most of Crowley's notorious activities were carried out after he had left. In recent years however, researchers have been able to take a more objective look at the Order and there is no doubt that whatever the true origins of Westcott's original authority and information, and whatever the truth about the strange personalities associated with the Golden Dawn, the combined genius of Westcott and MacGregor Mathers did produce a system of psycho-spiritual training containing a genuine and dynamic synthesis of the different strands of the Western Esoteric Tradition whose vitality remains unsurpassed.

Even Crowley has benefitted from a re-examination of the Golden Dawn history. An increasing number of specialists are now of the opinion that Crowley was in fact merely an early "hippy," and that, whatever might have been his personality faults and rather outrageous tongue-in-cheek way of expressing himself, his courage and qualities as a hard-headed researcher cannot be denied. But whatever the final verdict, the Golden Dawn tradition still survives, and some modern esotericists are busy updating the system, discarding some of its nineteenth-century exaggerations and supplementing it with new knowledge which the Age of Aquarius has been showering upon us. Thus, despite the human failings of the individuals who drew up the Golden Dawn system, it was certainly one of the Guardians of the Tradition. Anyone doubting the efficacy of the system has only to try out some of its methods, which have by now been borrowed by all kinds of groups and are included in many current books on spiritual self-development.

THE TEMPLE IN THE AQUARIAN AGE

CHAPTER XVI
THE WORLD OF THE 1980s

THERE IS no need to catalogue the problems which we face in today's world. The writer agrees with esotericists and others who declare that our planet has entered the end of a cycle. It might even be added that we are living a spectacular moment in the history of our planet. We are now exactly at the cut-off point where we can either allow the forces of devolution to carry us downwards or at least freeze us in the grip of materialism for untold ages, or else make the necessary efforts to attune ourselves to the new evolutionary forces which could carry us as a species to undreamt-of spiritual realizations and achievements.

A brief look around us will show that both these impulses are at work. There are forces which are working towards the destruction of the environment in exchange for temporary material gain; these degrade the noble aspects of the human being. At other levels, this degradation of human beings is being stimulated physically through the eating of denatured food, and mentally by the flooding of people's minds with low quality entertainment. This includes certain video and television material which reduce people's desire to think and affect them negatively by the insidious introduction of the darker side of the spirit into their subconscious. Certain types of video cassettes and popular music which incite and cater to satanic tastes are already in worldwide circulation and are available to young and old alike.

Not enough attention is given to the problem of mental pollution and its effect on the subtle levels of our environment. Anyone who has doubts about the polluted state of our mental environment only has to look any evening at the summary of the day's news on television. The "worshippers of Mammon" who are stimulating this descent into darkness through greed for wealth and power, strangely enough do not seem to be concerned about the cesspool they are creating for themselves and their children.

But all is not lost. Positive forces are also at work. At this particular moment in the planet's evolution these positive forces are no longer confined to the successors of the esoteric movements whose histories and beliefs we have touched upon. Since the 1970s, positive influences can be seen in efforts by various environmental, wholistic and other New Age groups to improve the quality of life on the planet. The teachings of many of the "New Age" groups are of high quality—unfortunately most of the people who gravitate around them tend to be collectors of information, "enlightenment" techniques, and/or "week-end highs." They either do not understand the need—and possibly the teachers do not emphasize it sufficiently—for structure in their spiritual lives as in all other areas, a structure involving continuity in practice, and the demonstration of a commitment to work regularly on oneself and with others of like mind. Once a workshop or seminar is finished, few work at making their seminar experience a part of their everyday lives, tending to forget what they have learned until the next seminar, which they may begin no further on than when they began the last one, not having consolidated the experience. For any spiritual progress to be retained and built upon, it has to be prepared and sustained by efforts to work on one's shortcomings and to live the Christ life in the sense this book has tried to indicate. It is difficult to describe the joy that comes with the understanding that a hurdle has been jumped, a barrier broken through, and that one has reached a new and lighter space, looking at the world through new eyes as if for the first time. For each one of us the experience is intensely personal and yet so very real.

The writer is sincerely convinced that if a sufficient

number of people answer the call of the Temple and endeavor to lead a life dedicated to respect for man and life in all its forms, the current they will generate will bring about the required links with the evolutionary impulses now at work within the planet. Perhaps this can stave off global disaster, or at least ensure that there will be enough survivors to carry the species toward the evolutionary blueprint intended for mankind. We would again stress that our generation has the tremendous privilege of living at a time of singular opportunity.

It must be stressed here that the Temple does not reject the material world or matter as such. On the contrary, it considers man's real task to be that of spiritualizing matter. Man was conceived to be the link between spirit and matter. The Temple is ideal for Western people, who need to fulfill their destiny not by turning their backs on the material or by decrying the spiritual, but in combining the two so that eventually the perfection of the archetypal world is manifested in the world of matter. When this happens, that much-quoted maxim of Hermes Trismegistus " . . . as above, so below," will be realized.

Arginy Castle near Charentay, Beaujolais today.

CHAPTER XVII

THE TEMPLAR TRADITION IN OUR TIMES

IN THE CHAPTER dealing with the secret mission of the Templars, it was mentioned that the Temple or the Eternal Tradition, working through groups or esoteric orders, manifests at certain critical periods in the earth's evolution. The instruments chosen by the Tradition come forward, carry out their mission, and then disappear. In accordance with certain cyclical laws, their successors will appear at another time and even in another place to revive and transmit the flame of the Tradition.

All orders today which consider themselves to be within the Temple tradition have been eagerly awaiting the resurgence of the Order of the Temple in the Age of Aquarius. Some esoteric schools, using another symbolism to describe this long-awaited age, describe it as the Age of the Hawk. That is, a time in which the ancient Egyptian Sun-God Horus will leave his fiery orb to swoop down to earth, bringing his powerful vibrations of Justice, Truth and Unity to purify both man and his physical environment so that the Christ consciousness can freely manifest in us and around us.

Another way of saying this is that the cosmic energies symbolized by Aquarius and the hawk-headed Horus will be released, pushing aside or transforming not only overt evil, but hypocrisy masquerading as good. All men and women alive will be obliged to face up to their responsibilities at all levels towards themselves, towards the physical planet and towards the Cosmic Christ. At such a moment it is natural that the Eternal Order of the Temple will have a vital role to play, working through all those who strive to be worthy bearers of its inner tradition through their lives and actions, whether as individuals or as members of groups and orders.

In the Tradition it is said that the real Knights of the Order of the Temple can be found in all walks of life and in all religions and faiths. Many of these Knights of the Temple await the moment when something or someone will trigger off the link which lies in their subconscious awaiting the call. It is hoped that this book will reach at least some of them.

Those of the Tradition who have been awaiting the dawning of the new age are agreed that it has now begun. They are also agreed that the impulsion for the resurgence of the Order of the Temple has been given, and that the individuals who have a role to play in this revival will from now on, and over the next few years, find themselves attracted to those orders or groups which will permit them to carry out their mission.

There is general agreement in esoteric circles that the first impulse for the resurgence of the Order of the Temple was given in 1952, when a group of genuine representatives of the Order of the Temple held a commemorative meeting on June 12, in the Castle of Arginy, the place where Hugues de Payns and his comrades first took their vows in 1118. It can be stated further that the actual resurgence of the Order of the Temple took place on 21 March 1981. On that date a small group of men representing certain affiliations of the Order of the Knights Templar met together somewhere in the Swiss countryside at an old manor, once owned by the Order of the Knights of Malta. They comprised nine senior members of their Orders who had been initiated in the esoteric oral tradition of the Temple, and an inner council of seven brothers, each a member of the highest and most secret level, and whose origin and identity must remain hidden. They were told that they had been brought together in order to pool their knowledge and spiritual abilities to reconstitute and consolidate the manifestation of the Order of the Temple in modern times.

These men unanimously agreed that given the critical phase through which our planet is now passing, they would work to unite various strands of the Templar Tradition so that the Order could awaken fully from its long slumber to serve once again as a torch of inspiration to men and women who felt the call of the Eternal Temple. Those who took part in this historic meeting have begun the task of reuniting the different Orders which represent the modern Templar tradition. This task has not been an easy one, nor has it been without birthpangs, since many Orders have clung to the old ways and do not wish to carry out the reforms needed to operate effectively in modern times.

Some branches of the Order have persisted in equating traditional forms with the essence of the Tradition and have not wished to renew themselves. Perhaps one day some of them may be reminded of what was so well expressed in Matthew 9:17: "Neither do men put new wine into old bottles, else the bottles break, and the wine runneth out, and the bottles perish: but if they put new wine into new bottles then both are preserved." The real tradition of chivalry, the ideals of truth and beauty, the nobility of man and the quest for the Holy Grail can never change, but the forms in which they are realized must change, not only to adapt to the circumstances of the times, but sometimes to give birth to forms which will be the precursors or prototypes of ways which will help the human race to one day live more fulfilled and nobler lives.

A core group of the Orders involving the individuals mentioned above has reconstituted and consolidated itself into a new Order which was formally established in 1984. This new Order is known in French as "L'ORDRE INTERNATIONAL CHEVALERESQUE, TRADITION SOLAIRE"(OCITS). This is translated into English as "INTERNATIONAL ORDER OF CHIVALRY, SOLAR TRADITION." The Executive Council of this new Order decided that in line with the historic destiny of the Order of the Temple, the headquarters of the Order should be located somewhere on the North American continent. The reason for this decision is simple. North America has become the source of most of the new impulses which determine the way life evolves on this planet. It is therefore fitting that the modern Knight Templar of the old continent should play his part in the Age of Aquarius by adding his inspiration to that which his counterparts in the New World will bring to the planet.

Because of the historical and cultural links of the Order of the Knights Templar with France, the cradle of the Order, it is natural that the OCITS should establish its first North American foothold in Canada, a country whose bilingual culture makes it admirably suited for linking the old world with the new. Work is currently afoot which will enable the English-speaking peoples of Canada and the United States to contribute the energy and pragmatism which characterize them, and to add these to the Latin qualities which have marked the Templar tradition, so that in this new world of many cultures the two will work as one. The new environment will provide the vitality and vigor the Order of the Temple will need to fulfill its primordial destiny.

CHAPTER XVIII

AN ORDER OF THE KNIGHTS TEMPLAR TODAY

THE BASIC AIM of the Order of the Temple today is first and foremost to assemble those men and women who, imbued with a sense of devotion and service to humanity over and above their individual interests, are prepared to assist our world successfully to pass through the present critical phase of its evolution in order that the Consciousness of Unity of All That Is, implanted in the planet by the Creator and revitalized by the sacrifice of the Cosmic Christ, can be realized within the allocated cycle.

The Order of the Temple will therefore undertake, support and encourage actions directed, *inter-alia,* at:

—Promoting those civilizing ideals and values which are traditionally associated with the notion of chivalry

—Encouraging efforts to promote the spiritual unity of all men

—Fostering the fraternity of all men regardless of race, color or creed

—Protecting man's physical, mental and spiritual environment, and generally improving the quality of life

—Disseminating teachings which will help to integrate the spiritual with everyday life.

Orders established to realize the aims of the Temple will differ on the details and on the degree to which they actually realize the implementation of these goals in practice. The following is a brief summary of what an Order in the Templar tradition should be.

An Order should aspire to be the very embodiment of the aims listed above, and to give concrete expression to its responsibilities within the Templar tradition and structures adapted to meet the conditions of our time and age. All its actions should be guided by the ancient motto of the Templars—*Non nobis, Domine, non nobis, sed Nomine Tuo da gloriam.*

The aspirations of the Order should be spiritual above all else, and it should not therefore involve itself in political activities. This does not mean that the Order should stand aside from the problems and harsh realities of our contemporary world, but its influence on society should not be through support of any political platform. Rather it should be through the inner and outer attitudes of its members that an Order of the Temple can most effectively intervene in the world. It will be how a Templar lives and behaves that will decide the influence he will have on those around him. An Order should strive to be a center of radiant light inspiring men and women to join in the redemption of the planet by the example given by its members in their daily lives.

An Order should make its members constantly aware of the mystical link which unifies all things on all levels—body, soul and spirit; visible and invisible. It should therefore be able to provide sustenance to its members who seek to realize the deeper significance of the Tradition established by the Christ. In this sense an Order should be essentially religious, not in the usual meaning given to the term, but religious in its original meaning, i.e. "that which re-joins."

Although the Order of the Knights Templar originates from a military tradition, the only aspect of this heritage which should be retained today is that rigor of spirit and self-discipline which will exhort the modern Templar to fight and conquer his lower nature on that battlefield which is himself.

At the heart of the Templar tradition is the Rule. The Rule should commit its members to strive to live in unity with and in service to the Law with a capital L. The Law is the Christ.

The Templar should live the Law through:

Order and Discipline

Honor and Respect

Loyalty and Obedience

The Offering of Self and the Exercise of Discretion

Consciousness and Love.

Order and Discipline

All forms of life inferior to man automatically follow the Law. Man, who possesses free will, rarely follows the Law. He should endeavor to integrate himself with that state of Universal Order through a freely accepted self-discipline. Order and discipline should be present in all activities carried out within the Order, whether individual or collective. They will be manifested *inter-alia* by:

Readiness to serve at all times
Economy
Concern for general and personal hygiene
Punctuality
Discernment
An acute sense of responsibility at all times.

An Order should encourage its members to preserve good health in body and spirit in order to be effective instruments for expressing and transmitting the Law which is also Light and Life.

Honor and Respect

Honor is that moral dignity and esteem which one associates with chivalry. Honor implies keeping one's word once it is freely given with full awareness of the obligations involved. Real respect is based on esteem and not on fear. This realization should lead a Templar to treat his fellows as he would like to be treated himself, and always to put the interests of his fellow-beings above his own.

If a Templar respects himself, i.e. recognizes the Divine in himself, he will automatically respect all manifestations of life whether great or small, whether material or spiritual, whether visible or invisible. Real respect exists wherever it springs from the heart. It is born from the expansion of consciousness which will make it evident that all is Unity. In this sense every act becomes a willing sacrifice—it becomes sacred.

Loyalty and Obedience

Loyalty within an Order of the Temple is expressed through:

Faithfulness to commitments undertaken
Honesty to oneself and to others
Perseverance and patience in the task
of realizing the ideals of the Temple
Constancy in maintaining the Templar Ethic
Courage and sincerity in the practice of one's beliefs.

Obedience facilitates the cohesion of the Order. It therefore implies objective participation based on trust and not a blind and servile submission.

The Offering of Self and the Exercise of Discretion

A true Templar lives and acts in the knowledge that in reality he owns nothing, in the sense that all the material and spiritual goods with which he might be blessed are only lent to him by Providence. These should be developed and employed altruistically for the glory of his Creator.

A Templar worthy of the name is aware that the joys and reality of Eternity are revealed in secret and in silence. As he discovers the reality behind appearances he will progressively possess the necessary discernment to offer the gift of self to the essence of things and beings, and not to the temporary illusion of their forms.

A respect for discretion and silence is therefore part of the Templar tradition, not with the intention of hiding or dissimulating anything but to:

Learn order and discipline
Learn to speak wisely
Avoid waste and dissipation of energy in idle chatter
Learn to appreciate that discretion enables one
to acquire more awareness and force in any action undertaken
Avoid profanation of the Templar Tradition or its Ethic.

Consciousness and Love

The modern Templar should be a conscious participant in the work of enabling the Christ Consciousness to return to its source through the spiritualization of matter. The spiritual consciousness of the Templar will increase as he or she puts into practice the teachings of the Christ, thus progressively becoming a living and vibrant stone in the edifice of the Eternal Temple.

The development and practice of love in the sense presented in this book will engender within the Templar a rich inner life. To the extent that this is achieved his actions will be automatically right, positive and constructive. The way of love or cosmic unity which was opened for us by the Cosmic Christ is the only possible way of return for humanity. Love once again is that quality which links and binds all life, all men and all things. It is that which harmonizes and transforms. Love is always present in its global unity, despite the diversity of external forms. Nothing can endure for long unless it is open to this cohesive force which reunites, transcends and gives life.

A Templar can never allow himself to forget that the mission of redemption transmitted to him by the Christ can only be achieved through love and respect for all creation, for his fellow-men and for the so-called lower forms of life, and for the planet which sustains him.

Some Activities of a Templar Order

A Templar is expected to participate in the activities of his Order in accordance with his conscience and his possibilities. He will be expected to work on developing himself spiritually and to take part in individual and collective activities to this end. He will be expected to work regularly in the traditional Houses and Commanderies.

A Templar is also expected to participate in certain traditional ceremonies which are performed periodically. There is for example the Essene Rite mentioned earlier, and the commemoration of certainly holy days such as Christmas, Epiphany, Easter, Whitsun (Pentecost), the Feast of St. John, the Assumption, St. Michael's Day etc.

The Templars, like many Orders, continue the old tradition of admission and initiation ceremonies. These types of ceremonies date back to antiquity when they were performed to formally welcome new entrants to the Mysteries. In fact the word "initiation" derives from the Latin word *initia*, meaning the first principles of a science. Later on the word initiation came to be used in societies or orders to describe ceremonies where a candidate who wished to advance further had to prove his readiness by successfully passing certain tests.

In genuine esoteric orders an initiation ceremony should in addition provoke a certain development of the candidate's spiritual awareness. A candidate for admission or advancement in a Templar Order will be tested in certain ways to demonstrate, among other things, his patience, persistence and desire to serve.

It is evident from what was said earlier, particularly in the chapters on the Grail and the Feminine Principle, that a modern Templar order cannot be a male preserve. Women are expected to participate in all activities on an equal footing with men, and consequently can rise to any level within an order.

It will be recalled that the Order of the Temple was abolished by the Papacy in 1312. Certain modern Templar Orders have tried without success to renew the link with Rome. Orders of the Knights Templar are therefore not sectarian and a properly ordained priest of any Christian denomination can perform the communion service in a Templar chapel.

CHAPTER XIX
CONCLUSION

IN THE PRECEDING PAGES, the author has given a brief introduction to the Western Temple tradition, the role of the Order of the Knights Templar in that tradition and the tasks and responsibilities of those aspiring to be Templars today.

In this the Age of Aquarius, the practice of keeping spiritual knowledge hidden is being abandoned quickly. Those readers who feel touched by the spiritual current of the Templar tradition will therefore have little difficulty in finding the necessary stimulation to enable them to realize their spiritual aspirations.

Such readers might feel that after so much mention of secret teachings in this book, I have left much unsaid. As mentioned in an earlier chapter, certain spiritual teachings have to be realized by direct experience and are therefore not transmissible intellectually, nor can their validity be demonstrated or proved merely by the written word.

To give a personal example, when I was younger, I read many books describing the spiritual experiences of others. While such descriptions did strengthen my motivation to continue the Quest, my intellectual comprehension of what I read did not change or transform my consciousness.

It is only by developing mastery of our desires, feelings and emotions that we can bring about that alchemical transformation whch will activate our psycho-spiritual centers in a natural way. Once these centers begin to operate naturally and automatically, intellectual comprehension will be gradually transcended by direct spiritual *knowing*.

Of course many books are now available which give exercises and techniques for directly stimulating the psycho-spiritual centers. In the Templar tradition, it is taught that these should not be stimulated artificially, but rather allowed to function in a natural way. According to this tradition, the present Age of Aquarius will enable this natural process to take place much more quickly than in the past, because the relevant spiritual energies reaching our planet are extremely powerful.

From this point of view, the only safe and reliable way to awaken our psycho-spiritual centers is to work on ourselves, guided by the ideal of service to our fellow human beings. Unless the centers begin to function within a context of systematic character development and altruistic service as they were intended to do, the awakening of latent paranormal powers will only accentuate our imbalances and distort our vision of the world.

People experimenting with direct stimulation of the centers often find that the powers they obtain do not make them happier because their basic problems of egoism, insecurity, hate, jealousy and aggression have not been worked out.

Against this background, I hope that this book will lead the reader to recognize that although life is to be lived fully, man was not placed on earth merely to pursue pleasure. The desire to serve life around us is our True Will, and denial of this is one of the fundamental causes of our discontent and unhappiness. We seek fulfillment in all kinds of objects and vain pursuits, and are surprised that no matter how much power or material riches we acquire, we remain unsatisfied. Real happiness comes from within after we have looked deeply into ourselves to discover our true ideals.

From a purely material point of view, it does not take a genius to realize that if sufficient people, while seeking the good things of life, also aspire to be of service, they and their children would live in a safer and happier world. For those who face financial difficulties, if they try to live lives inspired by true values, they will automatically attract circumstances which will improve their quality of life, and in the process probably realize that some material things they yearn for are not important anyway.

Assuming that you are convinced of all this, how can you begin the quest? Simply by:

—Reminding yourself daily of those thoughts expressed in this book which have set off a resonance within.

—Trying continuously to become aware that from now on every act that you perform, no matter how simple, is important, not just for your own evolution but for the whole scheme of things. You should therefore always try to be conscious of what you are doing and ensure that it is being done to the best of your ability.

—Paying active attention to what you read, hear or see, as well as what you eat and drink. This simple process will gradually enable you to develop discrimination as to what should be absorbed or rejected.

If these simple suggestions are put into practice, a difference in yourself will soon be realized. Example is the most convincing argument. Others will notice something special about you, and often even without any words being exchanged, they will be influenced positively in various ways.

It is obvious that the mass of mankind cannot change for the better by merely espousing an intellectual doctrine or ideology. Examples abound. The world can only be changed fundamentally if a process can be set in motion which will first transform our individual selves.

It is a fundamental belief of the Templar tradition, a belief backed by long experience, that if a seeker after truth begins to work seriously on himself, he will start to radiate light on the inner levels, thereby attracting to him all that he needs for his spiritual journey, including the appropriate teachers and congenial travelling companions.

Every man and woman who is stirred by stories, legends or

films of noble heroes is merely reacting to the promptings of that True Knight who sleeps within the heart. Some people pushed by this archetype become so fascinated with the nobility that they even spend large sums to acquire titles. True nobility of course does not spring from hereditary blood lines or honorary titles, but is a quality of the soul and must be lived.

The task of awakening the True Knight within us is not an easy one. We will need first of all to look honestly at ourselves and then take the first steps with courage and determination. The spiritual impulses of the Age of Aquarius will then certainly respond to the light of our aspiration and reveal to us that True Will which will guide us inevitably to the Grail.

BIBLIOGRAPHY

For readers wishing further details on some of the subjects covered in this book, the following is a short list of books selected from the vast range of literature available. Although the writer might not always be in agreement with some of the views expressed in the works listed, they are among the most valuable sources of published information on various aspects of the Western esoteric tradition. The writer is forever grateful to the authors concerned.

The Essenes

The Essene Odyssey. Hugh Schonfield; Element Books, Dorset, England, 1984

From Enoch to the Dead Sea Scrolls. Edmond Bordeaux Szekely; International Biogenic Society, USA, 1981

The Grail

Orders of the Quest: The Holy Grail. Manly P. Hall; Philosophical Research Society, Los Angeles, 1976

Mysteries of the Holy Grail. Corinne Heline; New Age Press, Los Angeles, 1977.

At the Table of the Grail. Edited by John Matthews; Routledge & Kegan Paul, London, 1984

Sur les Sentiers du Graal. Patrick Rivière; Editions Robert Laffont, Paris 1984

The Cosmic Christ

The Cosmic Christ. Violet Tweedale; Rider, London 1930

Les Grands Initiés. Edouard Schuré; Librairie Académique Perrin, Paris, 1980

The Mystery of the Christos. Corinne Heline; New Age Press, Los Angeles, 1961

The Rosicrucian Cosmo-Conception. Max Heindel; Rosicrucian Fellowship, Oceanside, California, 1966

From Sphinx to Christ. Edouard Schuré; Harper & Row, San Francisco, 1982

The Feminine Principle

Woman's Mysteries Ancient and Modern. M. Esther Harding; Harper Colophon, New York, 1976

The Time Falling Bodies Take to Light. William Irwin Thompson; St. Martin's Press, New York, 1981

The Cult of the Black Virgin. Ean Begg; Arkana, Routledge & Kegan Paul, London, 1985

Chivalry and Orders of Chivalry

Chivalry. Léon Gautier; translated by D.C. Dunning; Aldine Press, London, 1965

Les Mystères des Templiers. J.H. Probst-Birabeau; Omnium Litteraire, Paris, 1947

Les Mystères Templiers. Louis Charpentier; Editions Robert Laffont, Paris, 1967

Les Templiers sont parmi nous. Gérard de Séde; Editions J'ai Lu, France, 1971

Malta—The Maltese Islands and their History. T. Zammit; A.C. Aquilina, Malta, 1971

The Mysteries of Chartres Cathedral. Louis Charpentier; translated by Sir Ronald Fraser; Thorsons, Northamptonshire, England, 1972

Les Templiers. Laurent Dailliez; Librairie Academique Perrin, Paris, 1972

The Trial of the Templars. Malcolm Barber; Cambridge University Press, 1978

The Knights Templar. Stephen Howarth; Collins, London, 1982

Cabalism

The Mystical Qabalah. Dion Fortune; Williams and Norgate, London, 1958

A Practical Guide to Qabalistic Symbolism. Gareth Knight; Vols. I and II, Helios Book Service Ltd., Glos., England, 1965

The Tree of Life. Israel Regardie; Samuel Weiser, Inc., New York, 1969

A Garden of Pomegranates. Israel Regardie; Llewellyn Publications, St. Paul, Minnesota, 1970

The Tree of Life. Z'ev ben Shimon Halevi, Rider & Company, London, 1972

Concepts of Qabalah. William Gray, Sangreal Sodality Series Vol.3, Samuel Weiser, New York, 1984

Alchemy

L'Alchimie et son Code Symbolique. G.Monod-Herzen, Editions du Rocher, Monaco, 1978

The Fulcanelli Phenomenon. Kenneth Rayner Johnson, Neville Spearman, Jersey, 1980

The Cathars

Le Secret des Cathares. Gérard de Sède, Editions J'ai Lu, Brodard et Taupin, Paris, 1974

The Compagnons

Le Compagnonage en France. Jean-Claude Bayard, Payot, Paris, 1986

Les Illumines de l'art royal. Raoul Vergez, Presses Pocket, Brodard et Taupin, Paris, 1983

The Rosicrucians, the Rose-Croix

Les Rose-Croix. Sedir, Bibliotheque des Amitiés Spirituelles, Paris, 1964

The Rosicrucian Enlightenment. Francis A. Yates, Péladan, Granada, St. Albans, England, 1975

La Rose-Croix. Gérard de Sède; Editions J'ai Lu, Brodard et Taupin, Paris, 1978

Les Maisons secrètes de la Rose-Croix. Raymond Bernard; Editions Rosicruciennes, Villeneuve-St. Georges, 1979

The Rosy Cross Unveiled. Christopher McIntosh; Aquarian Press, Northamptonshire, 1980

Mystère et Mission des Rose-Croix. Jacques Duchaussoy; Editions du Rocher, Monaco, 1981

Freemasonry

The Freemasons. Eugen Lennhoff, translated by Einar Frame; A. Lewis Ltd., Middlesex, England, 1978

The Lost Keys of Freemasonry. Manly P. Hall; The Philosophical Research Society, Inc., Los Angeles, 1923

The Order of the Golden Dawn

My Rosicrucian Adventure. Israel Regardie; Llewellyn Publications, St. Paul, Minnesota, USA, 1971

What You Should Know About The Golden Dawn. Israel Regardie; Falcon Press, Phoenix, Arizona, USA, 1983

INDEX

Readers interested in joining a Templar Order should write to the author
c/o Threshold Books
RD 3, Box 1350
Putney, Vermont 05346